50 Tips
to
Help Students
Succeed

Develop Your Student's Time-Management

and Executive Skills for Life

By

Marydee Sklar

ΛGUΛNGΛ

Aguanga Publishing
Portland, Oregon

©2014 Aguanga Publishing
6312 SW Capitol Highway, Box 205
Portland, Oregon 97239-1938
www.ExecutiveFunctioningSuccess.com

ISBN: 978-0-9826059-7-4

To my children, Josh and Katie

You are living proof that, given enough time, the brain really does mature! Thank you both for all of your support and encouragement.

Acknowledgments

This book is an example of how many hands and minds come together in the creative process. It has been awesome to have my friend from Girl Scout days, Claire Ackerman McCrann, share her talents as the illustrator. Karen Marburger, writer and friend from college, graciously was my first reader and gave me confidence to continue. I also appreciate the time and effort of Nancy Loss and Fredericka Hoeveler for sharing their knowledge of neuroscience. It was great to work once again with my professional publishing team that turned my writing into a book: Kristen Hall-Geisler and Ali McCart, of Indigo Editing & Publications, Masha Shubin of Inkwater Press for the cover design and Ed Kamholz of Designs by Design for the book design. I especially appreciate Vinnie Kinsella at Indigo coming on board to wrap up the final design work when we needed his help at the last minute.

Of course, I could never have had the time to work on a book without the support of my wonderful team at Executive Functioning Success. They keep us all moving forward: Madeleine Wise, Erin Farrar, Kaye Sklar, Elizabeth Frommer, Josh Sklar, and Kat Wilson.

I am full of gratitude for all the parents who have shared their challenges and successes over the years. And of course, thanks go to my dear husband, Ron Sklar, for his continued support of my dreams and work.

Contents

one

Introductions: You and Me

Do You Need This Book?

All busy parents can use the tips in this book to teach their children the foundation of critical life skills needed to be productive and reach goals. This book is especially valuable for the following parents:

- If you have a child or teen struggling in school because of poor time management, planning, and organization, this book is for you.
- If your child has been tested and has a diagnosis of poor executive function skills, this book is for you.
- If your child has a diagnosis of ADD/ADHD, this book is for you.
- If there is a parent in your family who also struggles with time management, then this book is for you.

Who Am I to Write This Book?

For almost twenty years, my professional life has revolved around helping families of students struggling with poor time management, planning, and organization. Over many years of observing and analyzing their challenges and behaviors, I created a course that is called "Seeing My Time." Hundreds of people have now completed the program.

It is a unique course because of my unique background. First, I'm a teacher—specifically, a reading specialist. With this experience I have a solid understanding of the learning process required to teach effectively. Second, I spent the first forty years of my own life struggling with time-management issues. I understand the problem from the inside.

In fact, it was my personal success at changing my own poor time-management behaviors that set me on the path to write this book. Once I had solved my own issues, I realized that others—many others, including one of my own children—had the same problems with getting things done. Due to their inability to make good choices connected to using their time, these children and adults were suffering a lot of pain, like I had. It has become my life's mission to end this unnecessary pain.

As an educator, author, and coach, I speak nationally at conferences. I teach people about the connection between their brain and their time-management behavior. This is my third "Seeing My Time" book in three years. I train professionals to teach the "Seeing My Time" course in their communities and schools.

I am a busy woman, but my heart remains with those parents who still join me with their children. As I help them sort out their problems, I give these parents little tidbits of information on how to do things differently to better support their children. I share with them some of what I've learned the hard way!

I can personally see a limited number of families, and while I'm training people as fast as I can, I want to reach even *more* parents like you. I know that you are out there, worrying about your child's possibility for success. This book is my gift to you and all the other parents who need this book. Somewhere in these fifty tips is advice that will change your lives for the better. I know it.

What This Book Isn't and What This Book Is

This is not an academic book with footnotes and references to research about the brain and time management or what we now call an "executive function," a brain process that helps us to take purposeful action to get tasks done. Others have already written those books, and many of those books are excellent. You will find some of their titles in the back of this book. I encourage you to read them if you want more background on the topic of executive functions and behavior.

I want this book to cut to the basics of supporting the development of a child's executive skills of time management, planning, and organization. I designed it to be quickly read, easily understood, and very practical. I want the wonderful illustrations to bring a smile to your face, lightening your concerns and frustrations. I want to give you something concrete to do. I want to give you hope.

A Few Words about the Brain

Learning about the brain and its connection to our behavior changed my life. It has also changed the way that I approach helping students who are struggling with getting things done.

There was a time when a parent would drop off a child at my office and come back an hour later when I was done teaching the session on time management. I wasn't entirely comfortable with this arrangement. I suspected that while the child "got it" during our session together, he might not be able to independently use his knowledge. I wondered about his ability to use the strategies consistently on his own at home or at school.

It was while listening to a lecture on the brain development of teenagers that a light bulb went on. Teenagers' immature brains were at the root of the poor time-management behaviors of my struggling students. A child's brain needs years to develop time-management awareness and skills. I realized right then and there that to be truly effective, I needed to work with the child *and* her parents. I first needed to teach the parents about their child's brain and then about the time-management strategies that would support that developing brain. Adding a parent to the sessions was the key to helping the child become more successful both at school and at home.

Brain Basics

If you are like me and don't have a background in brain anatomy, it is easy to get lost in discussions about the brain. Here are five interesting bits of brain information that are useful to know as you move through this book:

1. *Executive function* is a term applied to many different brain processes, including time management, planning, and organization.
2. Our executive function processes are primarily located in our frontal lobe.
3. The frontal lobe is located at the front of the brain, just above your eyes. It takes up about one-third of your brain.

4. The last part of the brain to fully mature is within the area referred to as the frontal lobe.
5. While interactions within parts of the brain are very complex, our frontal lobe is often referred to as our "command center," the "CEO" of the brain.

A Few Words about Words

In writing this book, I got tired of writing certain words and combinations of words. Continuously writing *child or teen* or *children and teens* became tedious, so I simply use *child* or *children*. Please understand that those words are interchangeable with either *adolescents or teens.*

I understand that readers will often have either a son or a daughter who has challenges with executive functions. To avoid clumsy sentences with references to *your son or daughter,* I use a mixture of gender pronouns throughout the book.

Executive and *function* as a combination also become tedious. They get even more cumbersome when they become an adjective phrase: *executive function deficit, executive function skills,* etc. I decided to make it easy on myself, and hopefully on you, by using an acronym. Here's the code: EF or EFs = executive function or executive functions.

two

Start Here to Help Your Child

I wrote and designed this book for parents whose lives are crazy busy and who are going even crazier with a child struggling to get things done at home and at school. I wish that I could have read this book myself when I was raising my children.

I'm guessing that like so many parents, you have very little time to sit down and read. I've made my tips as simple as possible, with brief yet clear descriptions of the aids to use and the actions to take. You can read these tips in short, stolen moments of time, like when you're waiting to pick up kids from practice or eating lunch.

The tips and strategies are designed for students of all ages, beginning around fourth or fifth grade, when homework begins to be an issue. Some of the tips can be introduced to much younger students—and should be. Many tips are useful for adults too.

I want this book to make a real difference in your life and your child's life. These tips can bring about some major changes, but sadly, there is no magic pill or magic system to change your child's time-management behavior. Change will require some effort. But that doesn't mean you should give up before starting! You and your child don't have to live with constant frustrations, battles, tears, and anxiety connected to poor time management. You can make little changes that will support your child's success by building her executive function skills. Executive functions are those processes in the brain connected to our being able to get things done on time. I'll be discussing them throughout this book.

Change requires taking an action. So, try a tip at a time. Work with it; adapt it to fit with your family.

Write in This Book

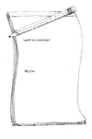

To help you focus on implementing a specific strategy, at the end of each tip there is a notepad for you to write down your action plan. Jot down what you want to remember from your reading. Record what you are going to do to set in motion the changes you and your child need.

The simple act of writing down your plan will dramatically increase the possibility of your actually doing it. In addition, put reminders into your phone or calendar to help you remember what you want and need to do.

Creating lasting change takes time. Be gentle with your child and yourself. Behavior change is a process. Create a little sign that says, "Little by little, change happens." Post it on the fridge or somewhere you will see it often.

The tips in this chapter give you very important background information to help you understand the connection between the brain's development and human behavior. Here, you will be introduced to the concept of executive functions.

Take a Deep Breath

Yes, right now, pause and take a couple of deep, calming breaths. I imagine you might need to. If you have a child who is struggling with time management and organization, you are somewhere between wanting to throttle him and collapsing in despair that he will never get it together. You are worried that you will be supporting this child for the rest of your life.

Have hope. Your child can get better at getting things done. These tips will help. Change is possible for all of your family. I've helped many families, and I can help you.

To begin, please read the rest of the tips in this chapter. Then read chapter three. The foundational concepts and tools you need to understand in order to successfully help your child are in these two chapters. After absorbing the information in these early chapters, if you want, you can look through the rest of the book and choose a chapter that addresses some of your more pressing concerns. Whichever chapter you choose, read that chapter's introduction before you read the tips.

 *Notepad*

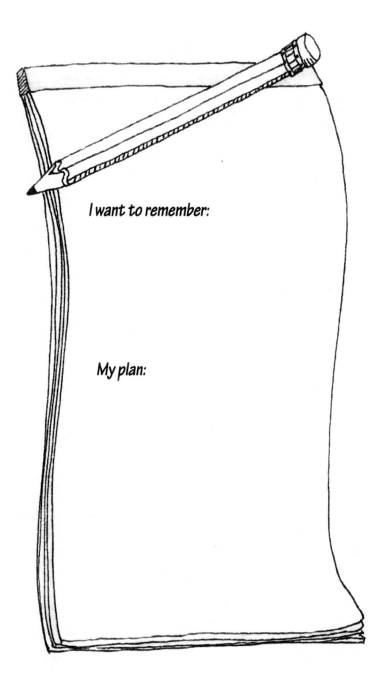

I want to remember:

My plan:

Blame
the Brain

Time management, planning, and organization are abilities rooted in our brain's development and its wiring. Our ability to manage time, focus, start tasks, finish tasks, plan projects, and control our own behavior are part of the processes in the brain described by neuroscience as "executive functions" (EFs).

It is important to accept that brain development is at the core of your child's challenges with getting things done. Everything that we ask a child to do—homework, chores, getting ready to leave the house, etc.—requires using the executive functions in her brain. Just as siblings look different, each brain's EF skills are different. Perhaps one of your children has no serious struggles with sitting down for homework, staying focused, or planning and completing projects. That child makes a parent feel powerful and competent. And then there is your other child, who, though he has the same parents and same rules, never gets anything done. Breathe. The differences are in their brains. Stop blaming the struggling child. Blame his brain.

Understand the Brain, Understand the Child

These differences in EFs are generally based in genetics and age. For instance, a child with a diagnosis of ADHD often has multiple EF deficits that get in her way at school and home. Unless there was an injury to the brain before or after birth, the symptoms of ADHD appear to have a genetic link. This link likely exists, diagnosed or not, somewhere in the near family tree and often in at least one parent.

If you want to know more about EFs, I invite you to skip to the appendix at end of this book, where you will find executive functions defined in greater detail. You'll be asked to evaluate both your child's and your own EFs to get a picture of each of your brains' strengths and weaknesses. This brief evaluation will help you better appreciate your child's brain and her struggles. Also in the appendix is a list of excellent books and resources that will expand your knowledge on the topic.

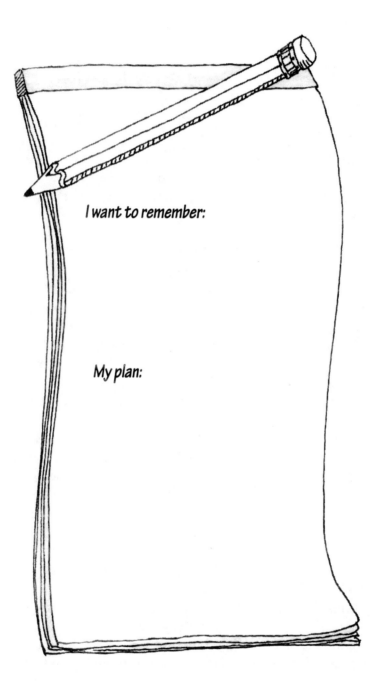

I want to remember:

My plan:

Age Is Key

If you have ever wanted to pull your hair out when a child informs you of an important project due *tomorrow,* you have surely wondered why your child did not plan ahead and avoid the last-minute trauma. The answer is simple: she couldn't plan ahead.

Your child's brain hasn't yet developed to the point where it thinks or cares about future deadlines. Young brains care about the present. The future isn't important, or even comprehensible. At best the typical middle school student is able to keep track of events that are several days away. For many, a deadline in just a week may get lost in the fog of the "future."

Brain science defines the EF skills that are required to think about tasks, plan tasks, and perform them as part of our brain's "executive system." This is a complex system involving many parts of our brain, and it develops over time. Different EF skills come online as we age. The executive system is the last part of our brain to fully mature. In fact—please sit down if you aren't already—the executive system is not fully mature until somewhere between the ages of twenty-five and thirty-plus years! That's right. It takes years and years to develop a fully mature brain.

This is good news for children struggling with getting things done. They aren't bad, lazy people; they are just young people. The problem for young people today is that we have raised our expectations at school and home. We demand completion of tasks that require adult EF skills.

While this is good news for young people, this slow brain maturation is bad news for you as a parent. You are going to have to help your child develop his brain's EF skills as he grows in order for him to be successful in school and into early adulthood.

The tips in this book will help you be a parent who is supportive of your child's development of EF skills. The skills taught in this book are life skills. They will help your child transition more easily into adulthood.

 **Notepad**

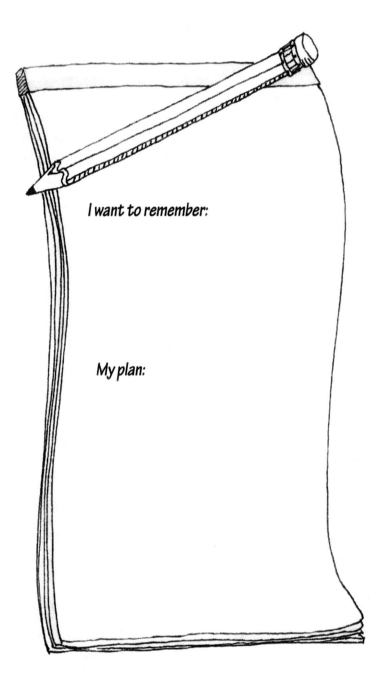

I want to remember:

My plan:

Change the Environment

If your child's brain can't internally monitor time and get things done, you need to change the physical environment around your child. The environment must support the weaknesses of a brain that struggles with tasks demanding strong EF skills. If you change the environment, the child can change.

If your child had an obvious physical deficit, such as requiring glasses to see or a wheelchair to get around, you would readily supply those supports. The trouble with EF deficits is that they are inside the brain where we can't see them. We assume that with proper internal motivation and willpower, a child will just perform executive functions because we tell her to. Wrong. You can't do what you can't do. You will need to provide external visual tools and strategies to support your child's brain.

How you introduce and teach the external and visual tools suggested throughout this book is important. I suggest you start with just one tip or strategy at a time. Introduce the ideas when everyone is calm and has energy, not when you are angry, and not with threats and ultimatums.

Start with Compassion

Introduce your strategy from a point of compassion, letting your child know that you get how painful it is to struggle with not getting things done. Show him this book and tell him that you are learning how time-management challenges involve the wiring in the brain and how you are learning simple ways to help the whole family.

You might present a few tips that you think would be helpful and have your child choose which one he thinks would be most useful. Explain why he needs to use a tool or strategy (because of his brain) and how it will help him (less stress over late work or missing papers, for example). Give your child some room to choose the tools so he's invested in the process.

It is also a good idea to think of something the whole family might work on. This takes the heat off of the individual struggling family member. You as the parent will need to model using the strategy or tool and, in the beginning, support your child by gently reminding him to use it.

In a way, you will have to loan your child your more developed brain while his develops. For a while, it is going to fall on your shoulders to support your child's growth toward independence. Be sure to practice using a strategy or tool over and over and over again. Repetition and practice will build your child's executive function skills.

If you feel like you could use some help becoming a more supportive parent, you might want to look at the resources in the appendix, where I list some options for building your parenting skills.

Don't forget: You can't do what you can't do. Your child isn't an adult yet!

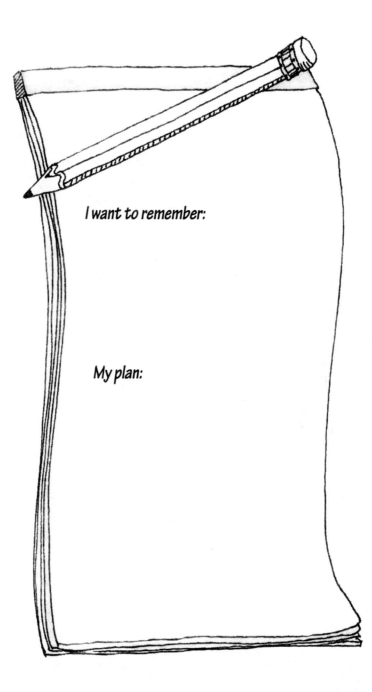

I want to remember:

My plan:

three

Time Tools Are Critical

A big reason your child struggles with time management is because of a fundamental problem with time itself: time is invisible. It is an abstract concept that we can't see or touch. Being unable to see time causes problems for those with EF challenges.

Your struggling, time-challenged child most likely has a brain that lacks an internal clock. If your brain doesn't have an internal clock, then you are in big trouble. You will be unaware of how the future is sneaking up on you.

Living in the present "feels" like you have lots of time to do things, so you don't connect your present choices to future consequences. For children this can look like choosing to play video games or read a novel after deciding that sometime in the future—probably at everyone's favorite time, "later"—they will work on homework.

This thinking gets them into trouble. They end up spending too much time on the video game or book. They are shocked when they've run out of time—and brain energy—to do the homework. While having fun, they are unaware of time passing. Without any external reminder for the passage of time, they will put off doing a task they don't want to do. They'll wait until the last minute—if they remember to do it at all.

Support the Brain with External Reminders of Time and Tasks

If a brain has internal EF weaknesses, including lack of an internal clock, then one *must* use external supports to get around those weaknesses. However, to successfully use external tools and strategies, you have to remember to use them! That can be a real problem, especially for people who have working memory challenges.

Working Memory Is a Key Executive Function

Our working memory capacity has a critical impact on our ability to do just about everything. It is very complex, and while I'm not a scientist in this area, I know a working memory deficit when I see it. Limited working memory is one of the most significant executive function deficits in my own brain. This makes my life tougher, because many of my other executive functions rely upon my working memory. No wonder I've had such challenges in my life! If your child struggles with working memory, she is also experiencing many challenges.

A Simple Explanation of Working Memory

You are using your working memory right now as you read and understand this book. Working memory is that part of our brain that supports "thinking" by holding on to information in order to process it. Working memory has a very small capacity and doesn't last very long.

I describe a typical adult's working memory as being the size of a three-by-three sticky note. It is small. You can't write much information on such a small space. Children have an even smaller sticky note.

The other thing to know is that our thoughts in working memory disappear in seconds. Once your sticky note is full, it is as if there is an automatic delete button that clears away old thoughts to make room for new thoughts.

This explains the child who can't remember directions that have multiple steps, so points are taken off her project grades because she left something out. This explains the child who was told to go upstairs to get his laundry but "forgets" to do that. This explains why I can't multiply double-digit numbers in my head. This explains why you find yourself standing in the middle of a room asking, *Why did I come in here?*

A Time-Challenged Brain
Pays Attention to What Is in Sight

One way to compensate for EF deficits is to make sure that all time-management tools are kept in sight. They must be easily seen to be effective reminders. As you continue through this book and begin using tools, pay attention to where you place them. Your child needs to be able to see them.

My First Truth of Time: Out of Sight, Out of Mind

In my "Seeing My Time" course for families, I teach folks to always remember the old adage, "Out of sight, out of mind." It is a great problem solver. If your child is struggling with time management and task completion, be sure to pause and analyze the environment. Make sure that time and task reminders are readily in sight. The tips in this chapter will help you do just that.

Analog Clocks

#5

The kind of clock you look at makes a big difference in the way you think about time. Most people depend upon digital clocks and watches. This is a problem for the time-challenged brain because digital clocks only show us one picture of time: the present, the time it is right now. The old-fashioned face clock, or analog clock, gives a much more useful view of time. It shows us the present, the past, and the future all in one glance. We get a visual view and reminder of the passage of time. The time-challenged child can see how long he's been doing something, such as how long he's been doing his math homework. He can also see the future and ask himself, *How long before I need to get ready for soccer?*

Analog Clocks Are Critical

The simplest strategy to make time concrete and visible for your child is to place analog clocks in all those places where she gets "lost" in time: in front of computers, next to the TV, in the shower, in bathrooms, where she eats breakfast, and where she does homework. I recommend small alarm or travel clocks because unlike wall clocks, these little clocks can be placed directly in the line of sight.

Make a list of where your family needs analog clocks. Write down when you are going to shop for the clocks you need. On my website, the "Cool Tools" section has links to a variety of clocks.

Be sure that your child can read an analog clock. Many young people, including some young adults, have grown up relying only on digital clocks.

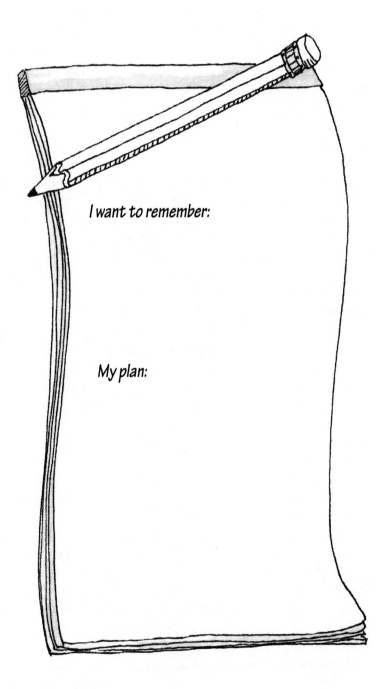

I want to remember:

My plan:

Wear a Watch

#6

Today a huge number of people don't wear watches. When asked why, they say they don't need one because they have a cell phone. Yes, you can check the time on a cell phone, but where do you keep it? It is usually in a pocket, or in a purse, or in a backpack. When the phone is out of sight and out of mind, the time is out of sight and out of mind too.

Since time is invisible, one of the best ways to "see time" as you go through the day is to wear a wristwatch. You want an analog watch, one with the round dial and numbers representing the space of twelve hours. This kind of watch, with its picture of present, past, and future, grounds you in the space of time so that you can make better time choices.

One of my children refused to wear a watch as a young adult. For years, every Christmas, birthday, and beginning of a new college term, I offered to buy him a watch. No, he didn't need one, thank you very much. He had his phone. Then one fall I got an email with this subject line: "Felt like a 14-year-old." He wrote that in class that day, a professor had yelled at him for taking out his cell phone in class to check the time. He provided the link to the watch he wanted me to get him. With one-click shopping, this mother was happy to send the watch. That was the moment when I knew he finally had an adult executive functioning system. Hallelujah! No longer was he stuck in resistance to a suggestion from his mother. Like an adult, he simply realized and accepted the fact that he needed a watch!

Before you go and buy watches for your family, remember these points:

- Buy analog watches, not digital watches.
- Don't buy a watch for someone else without their input. Watches are a very personal fashion statement.
- Adolescents especially have strong opinions about what makes a cool watch. He won't wear it if he doesn't like it.
- Make sure the dial is large enough to be easily read.
- Make sure it is comfortable to wear for long periods of time.
- Teach your child to read an analog clock if she can't yet.

One of my life's goals is to make wearing watches a symbol of being hip and cool. Get your time-challenged child a watch—and perhaps one for you too. Everyone's time awareness will improve.

Notepad

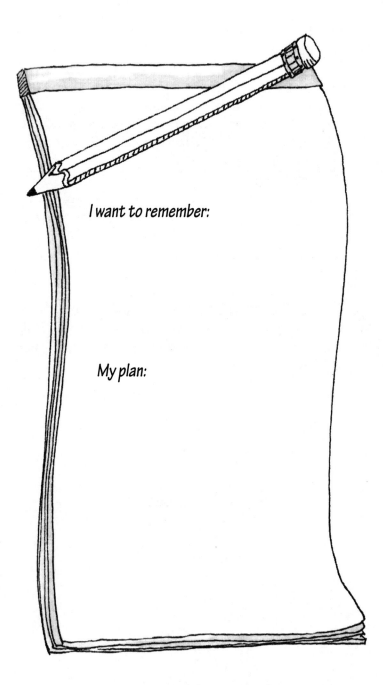

I want to remember:

My plan:

Whiteboards Are Powerful

A whiteboard is one of the best support tools for getting tasks done. It keeps the to-do list in sight, which can lead to awesome productivity and fewer family conflicts. I'm not talking about one kept away on a wall where people don't walk past it very often. I'm not talking about a small one on the front of the refrigerator. I'm talking about a bigger board, about two and a half by three feet, that is attached to a collapsible stand. Picture one being used by a presenter at a meeting and you have the idea.

My daughter taught me to use the portable whiteboard as a time tool. I had one in our dining room where I taught my private reading students. Each weekend she would take it over, creating a list of what she needed to accomplish to meet the demands of her college-prep high school. She would list each subject along with the time circle (described in the pages to come) to represent the estimated amount of time each task would take. She would always be sure to write down something fun to do too. That helped to motivate her to do the work. As she worked through her list, she would wander into the dining room and erase tasks or time circles to show her progress. It was great for me, because with the board in the dining room, I never had to ask her if she was doing her homework. I could see her doing it!

Use the Whiteboard as a Family Time-Management Tool

When I work with families, I recommend a whiteboard that can be used by the whole family to help everyone get things done. It works when it is kept in sight where everyone walks past it often. It folds up when you have company.

Here is how to use it:

1. **Assign every family member his or her own section of the board, perhaps even an individual color marker.**
2. **In their respective sections, people list what they both *need* and *want* to do on that day or weekend.**
3. **Estimate the spaces of time to spend on each task.** Visually represent that space of time with small circles that resemble the face of an analog clock. If it will take a full hour, color in the whole circle. If it is going to take fifteen minutes, then color in one-fourth of the circle. For example: if an event is going to take two and a half hours, you would draw two circles completely filled in, followed by a circle filled in halfway.
4. **As tasks are completed, cross them off.** This helps everyone see what other family members need to do and what they have completed.

Using the whiteboard in this way also allows parents to monitor the status of homework without constant nagging. Give praise as work gets done. If it isn't getting done, don't go to the yelling mode and make threats. Instead, take a deep breath, pause, and remind yourself that task initiation—just getting started—is an executive skill many children struggle with.

I recommend that you approach your child like this: "I was just walking past the whiteboard, and I noticed you haven't started your homework. Is there anything I can do to help you get started?" This approach is less likely to create a defensive response, and you'll be better able to determine if there is some point of confusion that you could clear up so that she can start.

The Whiteboard Is Not Your List for Them

This whiteboard is *not* the parent's list for the child or other family members. While you might be able to negotiate adding items to your child's list, he should be writing and checking off his own list. This is how independent time-management skills develop.

 *Notepad*

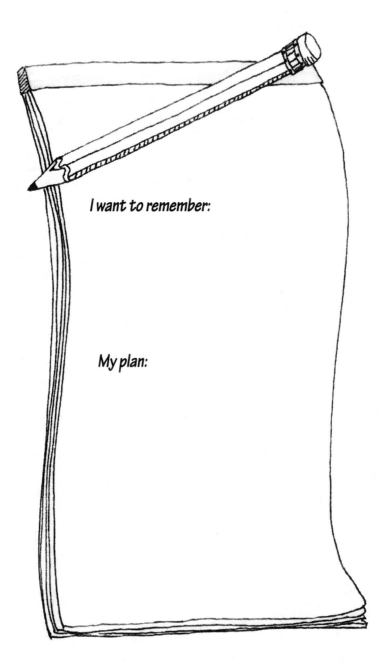

I want to remember:

My plan:

Calendars Are Critical

As a parent you are probably familiar with this delaying tactic: your child comes home with a project from school and says something like, "I've got lots of time. It's not due for a month." You urge her to start right away, but your message is not well received. At best, you are accused of nagging.

Part of the problem goes back to the brain. A brain with an immature EF system doesn't care about the future. It can't really even think about it. It is only interested in the now. Think of a small child in the car for a long drive. He will repeatedly ask, "Are we there yet?" Children can only manage a very short event horizon line. Unless they are focusing on a birthday, holiday, or the end of the school year, older elementary students might be able to track four or five days out. Many adolescents can only think ahead a couple of weeks. I once heard at a conference that most adults are only able to think about and track events three months ahead.

Calendars Connect to the Future

The problem is that students are getting multiple assignments that are due in the future—in a week, in a month, at the end of a semester, or even at the end of the school year! Students with EF challenges struggle to stay focused on the day-to-day homework and lose sight of those future deadlines.

The solution is to make the future visible by using monthly calendars. A monthly calendar not only shows the present date and a list of commitments, but it also shows a picture of the future. The picture of the time between when a project is assigned and when it is due is critical when it comes to meeting a deadline. Project deadlines on a monthly calendar creates a picture of the space of time available for the project.

Electronic Calendars

Today many people maintain electronic calendars, and while I am a big fan and user of technology, electronic calendars have a few serious limitations for time-challenged brains. For starters they are usually "out of sight" on a device, only accessible after multiple clicks.

In families it is often one parent who manages the family electronic calendar. This means that she is the only one who knows what is going on or what is coming up in the future. This makes her the default "executive functioning machine" for the whole family. This is a role that gets really tiring. The other problem with electronic calendars on small devices is that the view of the future is limited to the screen size, so it can be hard to get a clear, quick picture of exactly what is scheduled.

Large Monthly Calendars

I recommend using old-fashioned paper calendars. You need one that has enough space for each day to write down necessary information. A family calendar needs to be where it can be easily seen, not on the back of a door that is always open or in a spot most people just walk past. Some parents print off their electronic calendar each week and post it for the family to see.

Encourage your children to add events to the family calendar. They can have personal calendars too. In fact, I always want my older students to post personal calendars in their room—perhaps a printout of three months—so they can see the space of time over an academic quarter to help them manage the requirements of multiple classes.

You might also encourage your student to cross off each day to bring home the visual point that the deadline is getting closer. There are free downloadable calendars and planners at www.donnayoung.org. If you download a calendar to go into a binder, be sure to print it on card stock so that it will last a whole month without ripping out its holes.

 **Notepad**

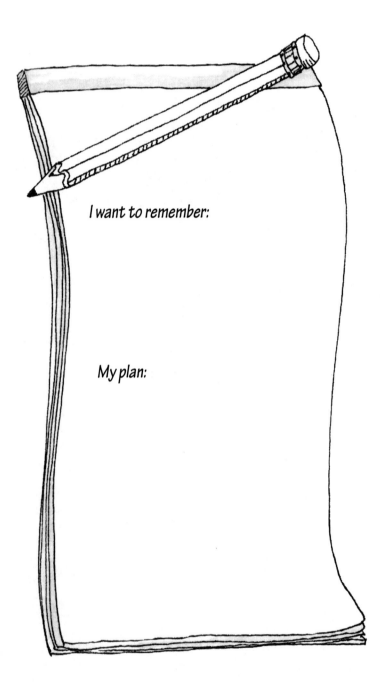

I want to remember:

My plan:

Terrific Timers

#9

Timers, specifically electronic timers, are one of my favorite time tools. They can be used in many ways to support the time-challenged brain.

Today we have many timer options to fit a variety of situations. A number of the tips in this book recommend the use of timers to help the time-challenged brain. Different timers meet the needs of different people and different tasks.

A Timer for Each Situation

I personally use four timers. One of them is on a string that goes around my neck so that my timer goes with me as I move about the house or yard. Another is a small portable electronic timer that is so extraordinarily loud and obnoxious that it makes an unavoidable reminder.

One of the most popular timers for me, as well as many of my students, is a cube timer. It has a terrific, simple design. To activate one of the four time choices, you just flip it so that the time you desire is on top. To turn it off, you flip it over to zero.

I am also becoming a fan of the clock function on my iPad, which includes a timer. The good thing about it is that you can leave a description of what you're supposed to do when the timer goes off. This function is great for those of us with working memory issues who don't remember why a timer just went off. In a school setting, my sister reported this timer was the only one successfully used by a student who is on the autism spectrum. The teacher scheduled in all of the necessary transitions, with descriptions of what this child was supposed to do at each alarm. The child knew what to do at appropriate times without the teacher constantly reminding the child verbally.

There are all sorts of other timers on phones, watches, and even your stove. As you consider the options, remember simple is usually better. You may also want more than one timer. When my children were at home, before the days of tablets and smartphones, we had at least four electronic timers around the house that were used by all of us. Links to some of the timers I've discussed can be found on my website under "Cool Tools."

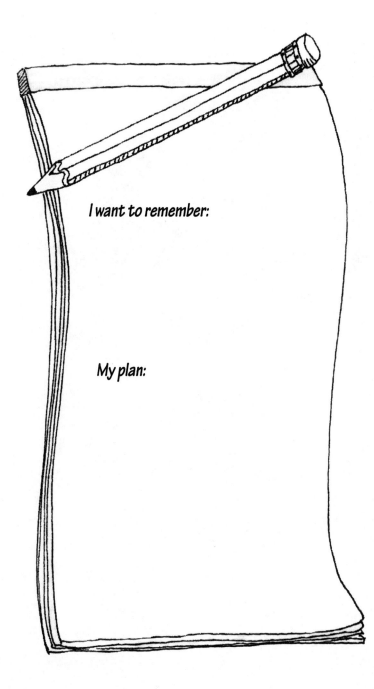

I want to remember:

My plan:

four

Hassles over Homework

Continuing struggles over homework is what typically motivates a family to take the "Seeing My Time" course that I developed. They have a child who isn't managing his homework and papers. Missing or late assignments are common, and grades go down accordingly. Frustrated and concerned parents then have their child tested by learning specialists, psychologists, and neuropsychologists. As a result of this testing, specific learning disabilities may be discovered, and weaknesses in executive functioning skills are usually documented.

After the testing, many recommendations are focused on accommodations teachers could make in the classroom. Teachers can and should help students with EF shortcomings to increase the possibility of the child's success; however, to be perfectly honest, there is only so much a classroom teacher can do. I'm afraid that you as a parent might end up frustrated, angry, and disappointed if you expect the school to "fix" your child's EF challenges.

Take Charge

A speaker at a Brain and Learning Conference on Executive Functioning and School Success told a very large audience that when it comes to helping a child build his executive skills, "parents have to be the heavy lifters." I've forgotten the name of the speaker, but I remember what he said!

The purpose of this book is to help you become that "heavy lifter." The tips in this chapter are directed at helping you help your child be more successful at managing his homework. Over time, with your support, little by little, he will become more independent when getting things done.

Ask Two Questions

#10

"What? You have a project due *tomorrow?!"*

If your child tends to surprise you with news that a project is due, you'll find yourself getting very angry and frustrated. For days (or weeks!), she hasn't said a word about it, despite your having asked if she had any homework. The problem may be because you haven't been asking the right question.

When you ask most students if they have any homework, they may be able to truthfully say that they don't have any or that they have gotten it done in class. And from their point of view, they are telling the truth. They think of homework as those tasks that are due tomorrow or in the next couple of days.

Projects that are due in the future are something else. It is as if in a student's brain, there are two separate compartments—one for homework and one for projects. From an EF point of view, this makes sense. An immature brain with EF challenges doesn't really think about—or care about—things that are out in "the future." Ask if a student has any *projects* to work on, and you might get, "Oh, yeah, I've got to work on the ..."

There are two crucial questions to ask every day if you want to help your child succeed with assignments:

1. Do you have any homework?
2. Do you have any projects that need to be worked on?

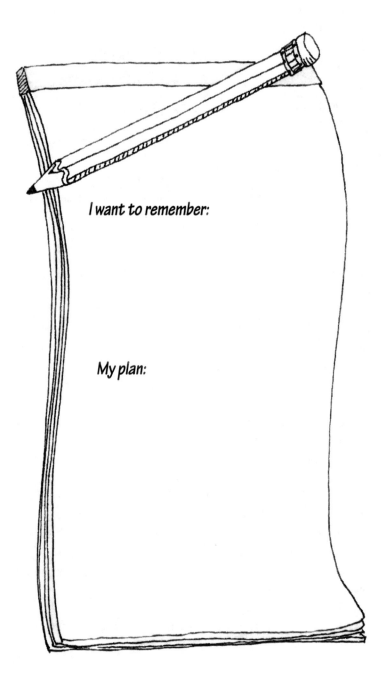

I want to remember:

My plan:

Get Papers Home and Back to School

#11

Many students with EF challenges struggle with transporting paper to and from school. Parents complain that completed work doesn't get turned in. Important communications from the teacher are never seen. Project descriptions are lost.

Everything Needs a Home

In many classroom settings, students aren't given adequate time to file incoming papers, so they just stuff them, which creates the opportunity for papers to get lost—out of sight and out of mind. Papers are lost in desks, lockers, books, binders, and the ultimate black hole: the backpack.

To solve this problem of getting papers home from school, all papers collected during the school day need to go into just *one* place. There needs to be one predictable "home" location where papers can be easily found when the student sits down to do homework.

My solution is to use a transparent plastic pocket folder, which I call the "to and from" folder. This folder is used to take papers to and from school.

Get Papers Home from School

The transparent "to and from" folder is placed in the very front of a student's school binder. It should be the first thing the child sees when the binder is opened. All papers collected during the school day should be placed into that folder. Don't worry about order at this point. We just want to get the papers home, in one place, so that they can be found.

Teach your child to empty this folder *every day* so that it doesn't become a new pile. In the beginning you will need to model how to do this. You will need to be sure that it is emptied every day, then deal with or file the papers where they can be found. Read tip #12 for directions on what to do with the individual papers and how to set up an effective binder for filing.

Get Completed Work Back to School

When an assignment is completed, it is placed in the front pocket of the "to and from" folder. It should be face up so that your child gets a visual reminder for that homework to be turned in as soon as he opens his binder at school. If there are multiple pages of homework, the assignments should be placed in the order that the subjects are taught during the day. For example, if math is the first class of the morning, it is the first paper to be seen. If social studies is next, then that homework goes under the math paper, face up, and so on. Once the math is turned in, the social studies paper will now be on top, in sight, as a visual reminder to turn it in.

The "to and from" folder is a tool that supports the EF skills of working memory and organization. Students often report that this is one of the most valuable tools they adopt after taking the "Seeing My Time" course.

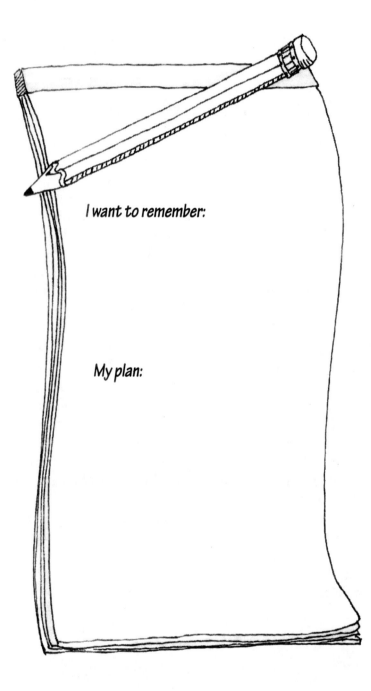

I want to remember:

My plan:

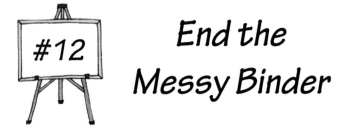

End the Messy Binder

Is your child's binder an out-of-control pile of paper barely contained by the binder covers? This is a symptom of a difficulty with another aspect of executive functioning: the ability to organize papers so a paper can be found quickly and easily when it is needed.

For a binder to work efficiently and usefully, it needs at least two components. The first is a "to and from" folder, which I described in tip #11. The second component is plastic two-pocket subject dividers.

Each Paper Needs a Home

Organize the messy binder by thinking of the binder as a portable filing cabinet. Your child needs to have a "home" for any paper she brings home from school that will be needed at some point in the future back at school. I recommend a plastic pocket divider for each subject during the school day.

If your child draws, doodles, designs airplanes, or writes poetry in class, those pieces of paper are important to them, so include a pocket divider for personal papers. If you don't, those personal papers get mixed in with everything else, destroying the organizational system.

Organizing an Effective Binder

1. **Purchase binder-organizing materials.** Get your child a transparent "to and from" folder and enough plastic tabbed pocket dividers for each subject, plus one for personal papers. You will also want quick-loading sheet protectors. If you need a mental picture for these items or don't want to make a shopping trip, there are links under "Cool Tools" at ExecutiveFunctioning-Success.com for ideas and ordering information.
2. **Set aside time for the child to organize his binder.** Once again, let him do as much as possible on his own so he takes ownership of his binder. You may need to help him get started. It's that tricky line of guiding without doing it all for the child.
3. **Empty the "to and from" folder daily.** When your child gets home, it is time to remove all the papers from her folder. That pile of papers can be divided into the following stacks:
   - **Recycle pile:** Recycle anything old that does not have a grade on it.
   - **Tonight's homework:** Set that aside but in plain sight, so it can be started as soon as this sorting process is completed.
   - **Papers for parents:** Some papers need an adult's attention—forms to be signed, notice of meetings or events, etc. If you create a home for these papers, your child can put them where you will see them and be able to respond in a timely fashion.
   - **File for later:** Some papers need to be kept for later use at school. These papers need to be filed into the appropriate subject pocket divider in the binder.
   - **Reference Pages:** These include any descrip-

tions of project assignments, rubrics for grading, etc., that will need to be stored and looked at repeatedly over a period of time. Place these reference papers into quick-loading sheet protectors and file them in the binder behind the appropriate subject divider. This will make it easy find those important pages during class or at home.

- **Graded papers:** Have a box or folder at home for storing all graded papers. This is for insurance. Teachers have a tremendous number of papers to grade and keep track of, and once in a while, one might make a mistake. Storing these old papers will enable your child to prove that a paper was turned in or that a particular grade was given if there's a question later on. At the end of the grading period, or year, recycle the whole pile.

4. **Support creation of the habit.** Every day for a week or more (depending upon your child), make sure that your child is regularly emptying his "to and from" folder and properly filing his papers. Once he's got the hang of it, he will realize it only takes a couple of minutes to do this organizing and filing. The benefit is huge. Gone is the frantic digging for a missing paper in class, which is a very uncomfortable feeling.

5. **Schedule time for maintenance.** To maintain the order, set dates on your family's monthly calendar for binder clean-out. Your child can do her binder and backpack while you do your personal binder or bag.

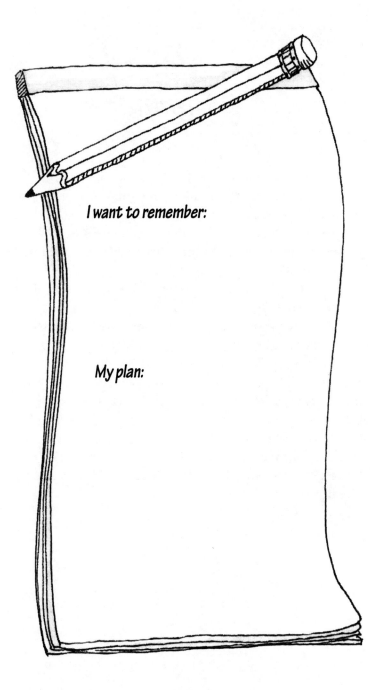

I want to remember:

My plan:

Digital Planners

Writing down assignments in the school planner or agenda is a real stumbling block for some students with EF challenges. Whatever the reason—poor handwriting, slow mental processing, or lack of focus—some students are better motivated and more successful using a digital assignment planner.

One mother reported to me that the only assignment tool her seventh-grade son had been able to successfully use was the iPad app iStudiez Pro. I purchased it, and while not a perfect fit for my brain's needs (the month view was too small), it works pretty easily and would be a good fit for many middle school through college students who have Apple tablets. Given the rapidly evolving world of available applications, I'm sure that one could find several other apps that might be helpful. Have your child investigate the options, pick one, and then show you how it works. It is valuable to have your child be the authority and teacher once in a while!

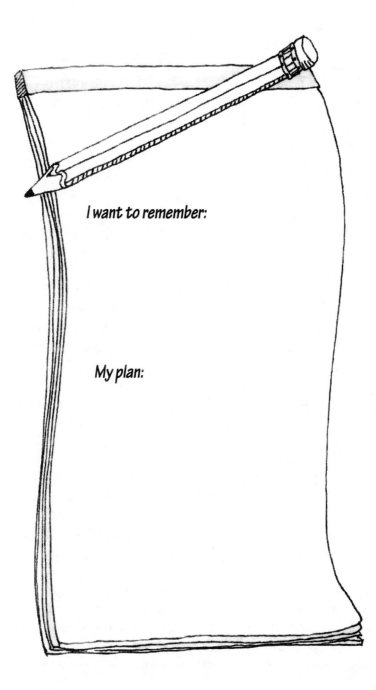

I want to remember:

My plan:

Assignments Posted Online

While many schools still distribute spiral-bound paper planners for recording assignments, many schools are switching to digital formats. The switch to digital presents pitfalls for students with EF deficits. If your child is being asked to access homework online, please consider the following ways to offer support:

1. **Learn to use the system yourself.** Don't assume that your child knows how to access his assignments online. Ask your student to be *your* teacher and show you how it works. With this approach, you'll be able to quickly determine if he does understand the system. If he doesn't, arrange to get help for both of you.

2. **Write down digital assignments.** Transfer online daily assignments to a day plan, on either paper or a whiteboard. Transfer projects that are due in the future to a monthly calendar. Students with EF deficits often have working memory challenges, which makes remembering sequences of information difficult. If your child has to look up multiple classes for homework on different web pages, she will never be able to keep assignment details straight in her head. Something will be missed or forgotten. Writing it down where the student can easily see it solves the working memory problem.

3. **Determine which teachers post assignments online.** As of this writing, not all teachers are consistently posting assignments online. This inconsistency

creates holes that those with EF weaknesses can fall into. They can't remember if the teacher said anything about homework. If specific teachers don't post assignments consistently or at all, be sure that your child has contact information for at least two peers in each class. This will allow her to have someone to call for clarification about assignments.

 **Notepad**

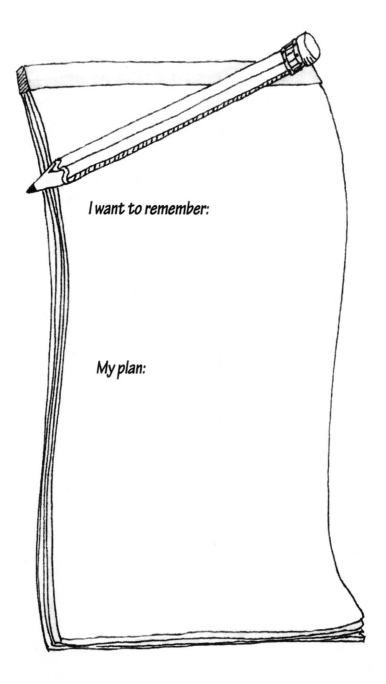

I want to remember:

My plan:

#15

Where to Do Homework

For many children, getting their first desk in their bedroom, is a sign of growing up. For parents it is a sign of the expectation that this desk is going to be used for homework. That is a lovely expectation; however, disappearing into the bedroom to "do homework" at a desk doesn't often work for a student with EF deficits. In fact, going out of your sight (and out of your mind) may be setting these children up to fail. A brain with weak EF skills can't control or self-regulate its own behavior to stay focused and on task while surrounded with the temptations of a room and the time wasters that suck us into an online world. For the child with weak EF skills, working alone in her room may not be the best choice.

Do Homework Away from Distractions

Determining the best place to do homework, away from distractions and temptations, will have challenges for each home. Family compromises may be necessary. Here are some guidelines to consider:

1. **Limit noise.** Create a time for homework with no TVs on and no radio. If your child demands music, make sure it is quiet background instrumentals. Avoid music with lyrics. Loud, stimulating music is great for cleaning rooms and hanging out, but not so good for the brain doing homework.

2. **Limit temptations and distractions.** Choose a spot away from easy access to phones and the online world. See chapter seven for suggestions on dealing with these distractions.

3. **Keep your student in view.** One option for homework time is to place your child with her back to you. This way, you can keep an eye on her computer screen to make sure she isn't multitasking. Another option would be to have your student working at one end of the table while you work at the other doing your own paperwork, emails, or reading.

When my own children were growing up, I didn't have this knowledge about the brain and its executive functions. My daughter could complete work independently. Not so with my son, although I kept assuming that he could and would. As a young person, my son couldn't self-regulate and avoid the temptations of distractions when asked to work alone. His grades suffered as a result.

Years later, when I had learned more about brain development, I told my son that I wished that I had set him down at one end of the table while I worked on the other. I also should have asked to see his completed work. His reply: "You should have. That's what the successful kids' moms were doing." Ouch.

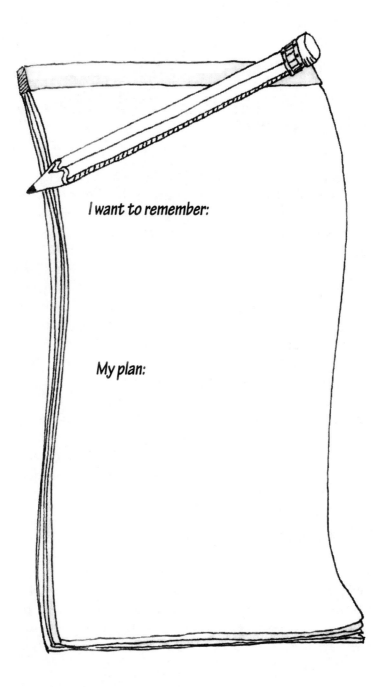

I want to remember:

My plan:

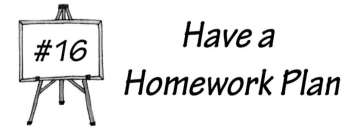

Have a Homework Plan

#16

Many children get home from school or after-school activities and make a beeline for the kitchen before settling down with their electronic entertainment, social networking device, TV, or a book they want to finish. (Yes, there are still children who enjoy reading, thank heavens!) Homework and chores are the last things on their mind. From a brain perspective, these children are not thinking ahead about how homework, dinner, doing dishes, and a shower are going to fit into the rest of their day. A brain with EF weaknesses tends to live only in the present.

To support a brain that only lives in the now and might be easily distracted, it is critical to create a plan for staying focused on homework and chores that need to be done. Children who struggle with EF challenges cannot keep a task list in their head. They need external reminders. These external reminders help a child whose brain energy is depleted after a long day of school and after-school activities.

A List Is Not a Plan

A to-do list is just a list. A plan, however, requires activating executive function skills in the brain. A plan requires being strategic with your time management. You must consider the space of time you have. For a student, tasks have to fit into the time before going to bed.

A plan requires thinking about the future, which means remembering to work on projects due in a few weeks, not just homework due tomorrow. A plan considers all of your responsibilities—remembering chores as well as homework. And a good plan motivates you by including a personal reward. Promise yourself a fun activity or break once the homework and chores are done.

Teaching your child to plan his time and tasks is a tremendously important life skill. It will only take a couple of minutes after school each day for your child to create his plan for the time before going to bed. Developing this habit will make his adult life so much easier. Reading this whole tip will take longer than the actual planning.

Teach Your Child How to Plan

First, I'll give you the detailed description for teaching your child to become a planner. Then at the end I'll provide a summary.

1. **Provide a tool on which to record the plan.** Good options are a small personal whiteboard or paper on a clipboard. The key is to make it easy to use and visible while your child is actually doing her homework.

2. **Set the time.** Set up a routine to make planning happen at a consistent time. It is easiest to create a new habit by anchoring it to an existing habit. For example, if your child typically has a snack when she comes home, creating the after-school plan can be done while she snacks.

3. **Model the planning process.** Initially you may need to demonstrate how to make a plan. You can start by creating your own afternoon or evening plan while your child watches. Be sure to share your

thought process, explaining how you are deciding what to do and how long it will take. This will model how to plan. Then prompt your child to consider what he needs to do, including checking planners or online assignments as well as filing all the papers brought home from school that day.

4. **The child writes the plan.** It is important for your child to be the one creating the plan, since it is about her time, not yours. Your child needs to take ownership of developing the ability to plan the use of future time. In the beginning you can encourage and remind her what should be included, but she should do the writing. This is not your list. Your child needs to write down the following on her plan:
   - **Homework assignments**: Write down each subject, not just the word *homework*.
   - **Projects that she needs to work on**: Write down the specific step that she will be working on today.
   - **Chores**: Write down specific tasks that need to be done before going to bed.
   - **After-school activities**: Include anything that will take available time away from homework.
   - **Something fun**: Your child should include something to look forward to once the homework and chores are done. Planning a reward helps to self-motivate and build the work ethic your child will need to be a successful, money-making, independent adult who realizes that work comes before play.

5. **Record the estimated and actual times for each task.** Accurately estimating time is a skill usually lacking in those with EF challenges. By practicing estimating and noting the actual time needed to complete a task, young people will be collecting data

to help them make better estimates in the future. Have your child guess how long completing an assignment is going to take. Write down that estimate. Time the task from beginning to end with a clock or stopwatch. Write down the results, and compare the estimate to reality.

6. **Cross off assignments and tasks when completed.** It is so satisfying to cross off completed tasks. Your child will like this part. As you notice items being crossed off, be sure to compliment him on working hard.

7. **Show completed work to an adult.** I think it is wise to maintain the parental right to see the proof that an assignment has been completed. This is part of the checks-and-balances system of family that a parent needs to do. By asking your child to show you her work—you don't need to correct it—you'll be keeping her from falling miserably behind by limiting the possibility that she is being less than truthful about homework being done. Monitoring day by day is much easier than getting notifications from teachers that work is missing. It is very discouraging and difficult for students to dig out from under lots of missing assignments. They feel defeated, which promotes more procrastination.

Planning Process Summary

1. Provide a tool on which to write the plan so that it can be kept in sight.
2. Set a time to plan.
3. Model the planning process.
4. Have your child write his plan.
5. Record the estimated and actual times for each task to be completed.

6. Cross off completed tasks.
7. Show completed work to a parent.

The first couple of times your child does this planning process, record how long it takes to create this daily homework plan. A lot of children (and adults) don't plan because they think it takes too long. Once you time the planning process, you realize that it really goes very quickly. And you'll discover that keeping that plan in sight keeps your child—or yourself—focused on getting things done.

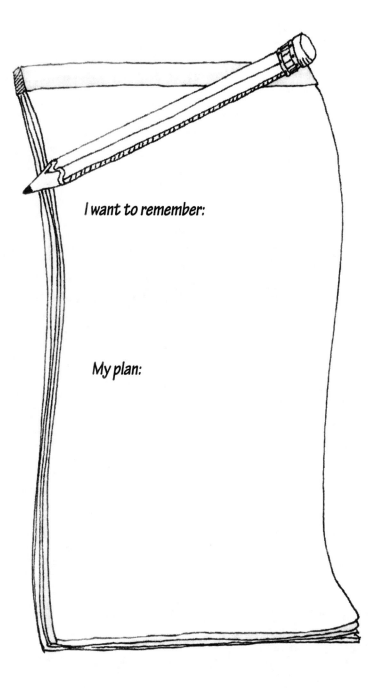

I want to remember:

My plan:

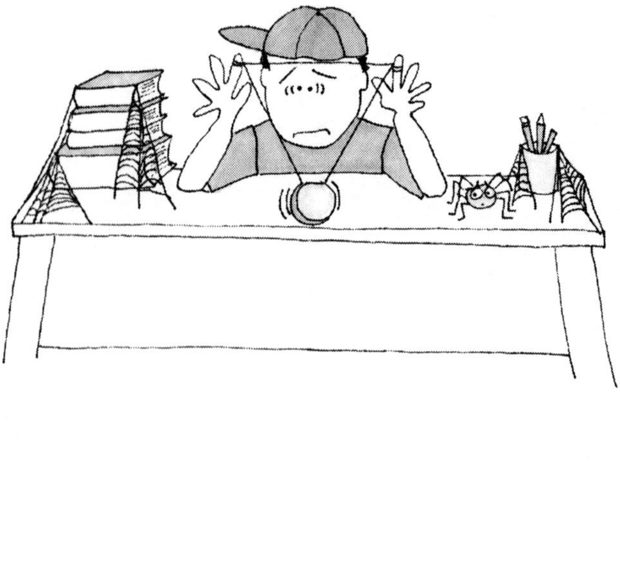

five

Procrastination

Children with executive functioning challenges are very often labeled as lazy because they have issues with procrastination and meeting deadlines. I want you to consider reframing how you think about your procrastinating child. It is not helpful to think of him as lazy; in fact, it is potentially harmful, as it can create a negative mindset within your child.

Let Go of the "Lazy" Label

George McCloskey, author of *Assessment and Intervention for Executive Function Difficulties*, suggests that children with executive function challenges are at tremendous risk for school failure, despite the fact that they may have no learning disability and may have significant academic strengths. Many of these struggling students are very intelligent, with high IQ scores.

When someone is constantly putting off beginning tasks, she is labeled a "procrastinator." This is a very negative label, and I know it well. For the first forty years of my life, I labeled myself "an underachieving procrastinator." The underlying assumption is that the person who can't get things done is just lazy. That is often not the case. Procrastination is more complicated than that. The ability to get started on a task requires executive skills in the brain and more.

To understand your child's procrastination, you need to appreciate what it takes for a brain to actually start homework. At the simplest level, it begins with brain energy, which is based on adequate sleep, food, and exercise. Then you need a brain that can stay focused on one thing long enough to finish it. And finally you need a brain with the capacity to delay gratification. These are all executive functions of the brain.

Starting to do homework takes even more than those essential internal brain functions. A child also has to actually understand *what* to do, have the *skill or knowledge* to do it, and have access to the *materials* required for the task.

In this chapter, I'll give you practical advice for several issues that may be stopping your child from beginning homework and projects. These tips will expand your ability to analyze the source of your child's procrastination and help her get past the barriers.

You Can't Do What You Can't Do

Not starting homework assignments often looks a lot like procrastination or being unfocused or unmotivated. Before you start another battle with your child over homework, I want you to pause, take a few deep breaths, and ask yourself these two questions: Where's the confusion? What doesn't she see or understand?

Too often struggling children leave the classroom without a clear understanding of how to do the assignment. They are missing some key knowledge necessary to complete the assignment. I think many assume that somehow when they get home, they will magically understand what to do. Instead of responding with nagging and anger, see if you can help clear up some confusion your child might be experiencing. Sometimes she is just stuck, and with a little help, she can continue on her own.

If your child is consistently avoiding homework, a critical early step is to determine if there may be an underlying undiagnosed learning disability. For instance, one in five children has some aspect of dyslexia, which means having a problem with reading: decoding new words, reading quickly and accurately, comprehending, and spelling. Some children have brains that need to learn reading and math with multisensory methods that allow for lots of practice. Not all teachers are trained to adjust instructional methods for learning differences. If you are concerned about a learning disability, I give advice for getting help in chapter nine.

Where Is the Confusion?

Help your child get unstuck by clearing up his confusion. He might not understand directions. He might not be able to figure out the first step of a multistep project. He might not understand key vocabulary in a question. He may not understand an underlying concept. I had a student not complete an assignment because he couldn't figure out how to fold a piece of paper into eighths.

Get Help

If your child is still struggling even with your help, or if you are getting into battles when you try to help, you need another person on the scene. There are many people and programs out there for tutoring. Interview people carefully. What is the tutor's background? What is her experience and education? You are looking for a match for your child's needs and personality. Also consider having your child undergo testing to determine if there is an undiagnosed learning disability.

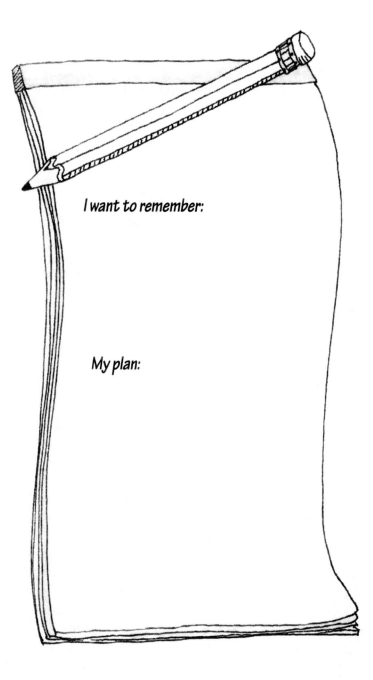

I want to remember:

My plan:

#18 Time Homework

Conflicts over starting homework are crazy makers. Parents often complain that their child spends more time and energy avoiding homework than it takes to actually do the homework. Sound familiar?

Once you've determined that the procrastination isn't rooted in confusion (see tip #17), you need to look for another source of the resistance. A child's lack of an internal sense of time can often be the culprit.

Step into the minds of children for a moment. They have been "at work" all day. It has taken a lot of brain energy to be in school. They have spent most of the day doing things that they may not have wanted to do. They want to chill. They want to have some fun. So naturally they fight back when asked to start their homework. They are guarding their free time. It is very likely that your child, with an immature EF system, is assuming that his homework will take up *all* of his free time. To risk starting his work, he needs proof that his homework won't take up all of his time.

A mind with an EF deficit connected to time awareness doesn't estimate time well. Unless a time-challenged person has collected some data based on past experience, any estimate she makes is just pulling a number out of the air.

You can collect this data any time of the year, but it is especially helpful at the beginning of a term when the child has new subjects and new teachers.

Develop Time-Estimating Skills

Being able to make educated estimates connected to the time required to do a task is another of those life skills that adults need. Here's how to help your child understand how to become a good estimator:

1. **Make a list.** At homework time, sit down with your child and have her make a list of homework assignments.
2. **Make a guess.** Next to each assignment, have your child make a guess as to how long each one will take.
3. **Time the assignment.** As he starts an assignment, have him either write down the time he begins or start a stopwatch timer.
4. **Don't allow multitasking.** To get the cleanest data, you need to assure that your child isn't multitasking while doing homework. Answering texts, playing games, choosing a song from a playlist, watching YouTube, and surfing the web are all multitasking activities that take up a lot of time. It would be a good idea to stay close at hand and monitor, perhaps indirectly. You might have her work at the dining room table. At the same time and at the same table, you should do something that you have been avoiding, like working on taxes or balancing your checkbook. You can set an example by timing how long it takes you to do your work. See tip #30 for more on multitasking.
5. **Record and compare.** Once a specific homework assignment is completed, your child should record the ending time and determine just how long that assignment took, then compare his estimate to reality. Do this for all the subjects, and repeat the timing exercise a few times so that you can create an average time needed for the homework in different subjects.

Usually a child discovers that homework goes faster than she thought, especially if she is not multitasking. Encourage her to take this knowledge and motivate herself to get the work done first so that she can play or relax in peace.

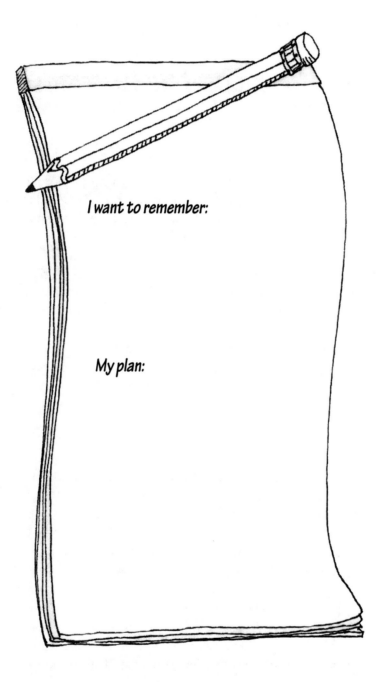

I want to remember:

My plan:

#19 Stop the Excuses

The classic excuse for not starting something is not having what's needed: "I left my book at school," or "I don't have a copy of the novel yet," or "I don't have the stuff I need for a display," or "I lost the directions."

To stop these excuses from happening, you must do some planning. Anticipate the kind of holes your child with EF deficits is likely to fall into during the school year. Your goal is to build your child's awareness of the value of planning ahead. When implementing strategies, be sure to talk about them with your child. Point out that by remembering past negative experiences, we can make choices to problem solve now to avoid future frustrations.

Useful Solutions for Typical Excuses

1. **Textbooks left at school:** I wholeheartedly suggest purchasing an extra set of key textbooks just for home. At the end of the year, you can sell them back to Amazon.
2. **I still don't have the novel:** At the beginning of the year or term, ask teachers for a reading list and order all the books. If your child is a slow reader, also get an audio-book version so he can listen to it.
3. **Don't have the supplies needed:** During back-to-school sales, get new markers, a couple of sheets of poster board, and a tri-fold display. Buy removable

labels that can be fed through your printer so your child won't have to worry about neat handwriting on the display. A pad of graph paper can also be handy.

4. **Missing project or assignment directions:** At the beginning of the year, be sure your child has a dependable study buddy who can scan or use his cell phone to take a picture of his copy of the directions and email them to your child. Of course, asking the teacher to email a copy might be possible. Store the directions in a sheet protector in your student's binder so that they can be found quickly amidst the other papers.

Notepad

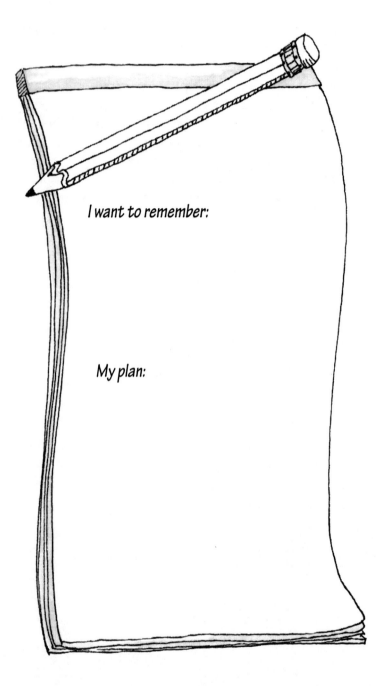

I want to remember:

My plan:

#20 *Starting Writing Assignments*

To sit down and create an original piece of writing requires a whole host of executive functions: time management, goal-directed persistence, planning, focus, and working memory, to name the obvious skills. The less obvious EF skill is organization. The challenge is to organize a disorganized mind to start writing.

Let's say that your child is given an assignment that requires doing research before composing a written paper. Collecting information from multiple sources is a very difficult task if you have a brain that struggles with organization. You have to take notes on appropriate information and keep track of all those notes. You then have to combine all that information into an original work that makes sense when it is read. You have to organize it, or sequence it, into a structure with a beginning, middle, and end. You have to be able to organize words into clear, original sentences and those sentences into paragraphs that have topic sentences and supporting details. Whew! It is hard. I know.

Writing was one of my biggest challenges in school. I avoided it whenever possible. My brain just couldn't internally organize all of the information collected on index cards or the ideas floating in my head. I couldn't figure out how to begin or where to begin, so I didn't. It looked like procrastination, but it wasn't. I couldn't do what I couldn't do.

Now I write all the time. This is my third book. Did my brain change? No. How I approached the task of writing changed. I started using my brain's visual strengths. For longer works, I don't start with the sentences (or outlines made up of word phrases). I start with an external picture of what I need to say. To do this, I either draw pictures or use computer applications to create mind maps. Once I've got the big picture down, the sentences flow out easily.

Visual Organizers Are a Great Tool

Visual organizers help create a picture of what you are going to write. They support the critical prewriting stage that so many students leave out.

While I will use paper and pencil for simple writing projects, I use computer software and apps for more complicated projects. There are many mind-mapping tools on the market, but my favorite is Inspiration software. It has multiple templates already organized to handle the typical writing assignments of school. You need to write a compare-and-contrast paper? They've got a template. Need to write a persuasive essay? Inspiration has you covered. Need to write a paper analyzing an event in history? It is there. Inspiration is easy to use. It even has a bank of clip art images so you don't have to draw. With one click or touch, you can turn an image template into a word outline. I love the app they created for the iPad. In fact, I organized this whole book and kept track of my progress using Inspiration on my iPad Mini.

Have Compassion for Struggling Writers

Use tools and strategies to help children see the order of what to write before actually starting to write. If they get stuck writing a sentence, suggest drawing a little cartoon picture of what they are thinking they want to write. Pictures and images are helpful for holding thoughts while writing. The pictures support working memory.

Notepad

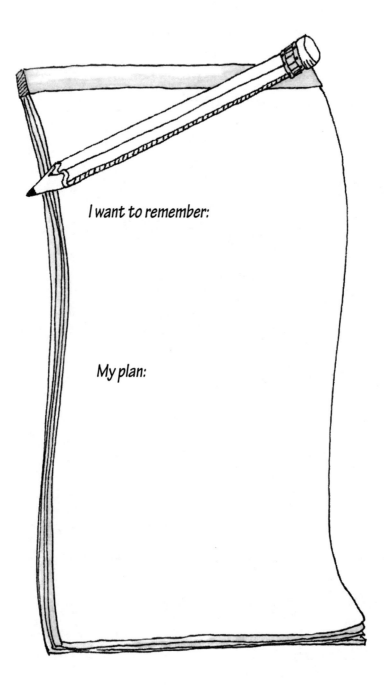

I want to remember:

My plan:

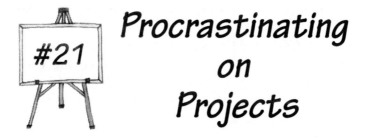

Procrastinating on Projects

Many time-challenged minds think best in images and pictures. These minds may also have limitations in the capacity of their working memory, a critical aspect of executive functioning. And they tend to live in the now, without connecting today's choices to future consequences. These traits all contribute to the failure of many students when it comes to completing and turning in projects on time. They will procrastinate and start too late to turn in quality work.

Imagine your child coming home with a project assignment that has multiple pages describing the teacher's expectations. The sheer number of words easily overwhelms the working memory capacity of the brain. This means that even though the teacher may have described the assignment and perhaps even read it to the students, your child will remember very few details. Procrastination often results because your child doesn't really have a clear understanding, or clear picture, of just what she needs to have done over a period of time.

Remember, your struggling child has a brain that cannot connect present actions to future outcomes. The distant future is impossible for her to grasp. She imagines lots and lots of future space to work on the project, so she ignores it for now. And she will argue with you about beginning the project, saying things like, "It isn't due for a month! I've got lots of time."

Her procrastination feels supported because it is very likely she dosen't understand all of the details of what needs to be done. She doesn't have a clear picture in her head of all the expectations and all the steps that have to be completed. She either imagines it is going to be really easy and fast to complete, or she is full of dread and anxiety over not doing it well, so she avoids starting. Either way, it becomes the motive for procrastination.

Get a Clear Picture of the Teacher's Expectations

To develop a clear picture of the project, the student needs to take some time, approximately thirty to sixty minutes, to translate all of those words in the instructions into images, bullet points, and dates on monthly calendars. Once this step is completed, you and your child will have a picture of all the other steps that have to be done. You will be teaching him how to connect with the future!

This process will support the limitations of working memory. Breaking those sentences from the directions into smaller pieces or pictures and recording them in another location is critical. You can use paper or a digital mind-mapping tool like Inspiration software. When you are done, you'll have a nice visual checklist of the whole project and a clear understanding of where you need to start. With a picture of the complexity and due dates on a monthly calendar, procrastination often disappears.

Break Directions into Steps

Teach your child to use this strategy on the very day that the project is assigned. Every day she waits to get this picture leaves fewer days to work on the pieces of the project, adding to the stress of procrastination.

Get a Picture of the Steps

Materials: Assignment/project directions, pencil, high-lighter pen, a blank piece of paper.

★Optional: Inspiration software on your computer or the Inspiration app for the iPad

Read tip #20 for more information about Inspiration software.

1. **On the project directions,** using a pencil, go through and circle every one of the following words and punctuation marks:
   - and
   - should include
   - must include
   - has to have
   - commas
   - periods
   - colons and semicolons

   Doing this will support working memory deficits. Complex sentences create multiple pictures in the mind, and when you have too many pictures or ideas, it is easy to forget something.
2. **Read directions aloud, clause by clause,** stopping at all circled words and punctuation marks. Perform steps #3 and #4 before moving on to the next clause.
3. **On a blank, unlined piece of paper★,** have your child draw what those words he just read aloud make him see in his mind. For example, if the words are *This project will be a written report on Egyptian pyramids,* then the child might draw a rectangle representing a piece of paper with little squiggly lines representing written words on a page and include a little drawing of a simple pyramid.

If you can symbolically draw something, you understand it. Drawing symbolic images of all of the topics
will help your child see all of the parts of the larger
project. For some directions, at a certain point, it will
make sense to just create a bullet-pointed list below
the topic image. For example, in the case of the report
on pyramids, under the drawn image there can be a
bullet list for all of the content expected by the teacher:
- Where built?
- Why built?
- Building materials
- etc.

*Instead of creating this picture on paper, your child
can use Inspiration software to make a digital picture.

4. **Once the sentence or clause has been drawn,** use
a highlighter pen to emphasize the words that have
been recorded in the drawing. This strategy prevents
getting lost in the directions and makes sure that your
child doesn't skip something by accident.

5. **Proceed through the directions,** pausing, drawing, or writing bullet points, and highlighting drawn
and recorded words as you go. Once this is finished,
both you and your child will be clear on what has to
be done. You can help him begin to see the chunks
or steps that are going to be required to complete this
writing assignment. The guessing is gone.

By doing this the very day the assignment comes home,
there is time to ask the teacher for clarification if the directions are confusing, which can sometimes happen. It feels
awful to be confused about directions the night before an
assignment is due but you can't get in touch with the teacher!

When you are done with this drawing out of the assignment, be sure to congratulate your student, because she has
already started working on that project!

Once you've done this "picturing" strategy a couple of times with your child, she should be able to independently create the steps for familiar projects as well as calculate a reasonable estimate of the time required for completion. Do come back to this strategy if a larger, more complex, or unfamiliar project shows up.

Notepad

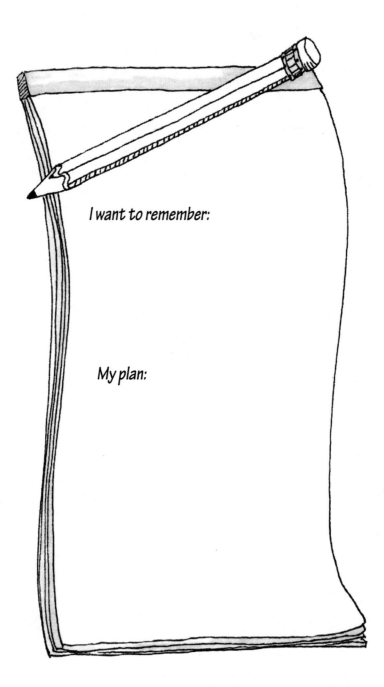

I want to remember:

My plan:

six

Conflicts Beyond Homework

While homework and time-management struggles cause most families to see me for help, it doesn't take long for parents to voice other frustrations:

- "She has to be nagged to do her chores."
- "He spends too much time playing video games."
- "Her room is a disaster."
- "We get into last-minute battles because of conflicts over plans."

If you have conflicts such as these, this chapter is for you. Once again, I recommend that you pause and take a deep breath. These annoying behaviors are tied to the brain development of your child. The good news is that you can support him or her to change and develop more positive habits.

The tips in this chapter can smooth out some typical conflicts and concerns. I created separate chapters for conflicts over distractions and chores, chapters seven and eight.

#22 A More Peaceful Week in Fifteen Minutes

A "house on wheels" describes many families. Parents and children often have very active lives that require some pretty complex organizing to get everyone where they need to be.

All that organizing and calendar keeping tends to land on the shoulders of one of the adults in the family. I call this person the family's "executive functioning machine." They know what's scheduled, while the rest of the family may not know or remember. The executive functioning machine needs to give family members advance warning to avoid the conflicts that often occur, especially with teenagers, when plans clash because of neglected communication.

Weekly Meetings

I remember working with a mother and her sixteen-year-old daughter who were in such constant conflict with each other that sessions were difficult to conduct. The way they talked to and about each other was not healthy or appropriate. After five sessions I sent them out the door with a referral for family counseling. When they returned a few weeks later to continue our sessions, they walked in the door as changed people. They were smiling and joking with each other. I thought, *Wow, that counselor is a miracle worker.*

When I asked the mom what strategies had been working well, she quickly responded, "The weekly family meeting." She explained that it was preventing fights and conflicts over scheduling. They had done it every Sunday. She then paused and said, "Except for last Sunday. It was a crazy day." Then she paused again, and a light bulb switched on in her head. She turned to her daughter and said, "Because we didn't meet last week, you didn't know about this meeting with Marydee this morning. And when I told you, we got into a big fight. You were all upset and angry because you had made plans for breakfast with your dad." Looking at both of us, she said, "We're going back to those Sunday family meetings."

Develop the routine of a ten-to-fifteen minute scheduled weekly family meeting. This has been a game changer for families, eliminating a lot of stress and conflict.

Keep It Simple and Fast

1. **Set a scheduled time and day.** Choose a day and time that will work most consistently for all the family members. Put meeting reminders into everyone's electronic devices and on the family wall calendar. See tip #8 for more about wall calendars.
2. **Gather everyone together.** Each family member should bring his or her own calendar (electronic or paper) and planner or assignment book.
3. **Everyone shares.** Each family member has a turn sharing their plans and needs for the coming week. Iron out conflicts at this meeting. Ask about school projects and if parent support is needed. Your meeting shouldn't take fifteen minutes. You might have a child time how long a family meeting takes.
4. **Update the family wall calendar.** This calendar provides quick-and-easy access to see all family commitments for the week, even if the family's executive function machine isn't available.

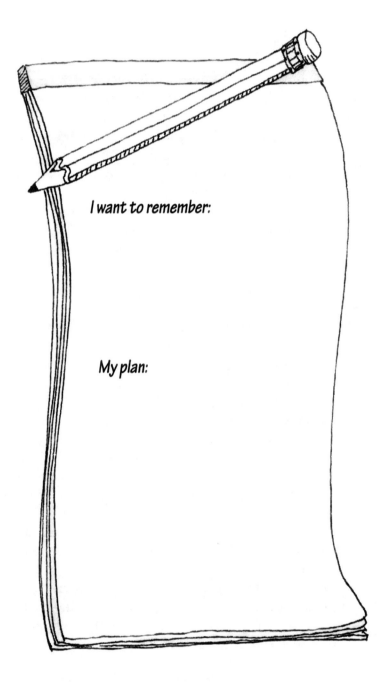

I want to remember:

My plan:

Set Up Routines

Remembering things like doing chores or where you put your backpack requires brain energy that engages multiple EF processes. Such "simple" things are not so simple for a child with an immature brain.

One way to help a struggling child with executive function deficits is to work around the weaknesses by using other areas and pathways in the brain. You can do that by creating routines.

Developing routines is a powerful aid for EF deficits. When we perform tasks over and over, like brushing our teeth morning and night, we don't have to think about it much at all. We just do it. When we have a habit or routine well established, it doesn't require as much active thought to do the task. Our prefrontal cortex doesn't have to engage as much. It takes less energy. Other automatic neural pathways take over the work.

Develop Routines to Avoid Conflicts

Take a minute or two and think about the conflicts you are having with your child. Is it getting out of the house in the morning? Is it getting ready for soccer? Is it helping with the dishes? Is it cleaning his room? Is it starting homework?

Start with one point of conflict and consider the following:

1. **Does my child *really* have a clear picture of all the steps required to meet my expectations?** Ask her to either tell you or draw for you the sequence of steps that she needs to complete. You might be surprised at what she leaves out. Multiple-step tasks require good working memory, which most children with EF deficits don't have. If your child is missing steps, the next thing for you to do is to effectively teach her what she needs to do. I emphasize *effectively teach* because very often we think teaching is telling someone what to do once or twice. If we have to repeat ourselves a third time, we get frustrated. Please see tip #34 for an excellent approach to teaching a multistep task.

2. **Does my child actually know how long a task is going to take?** Those with EF challenges don't have an internal understanding of time. They imagine that those "I don't like to do it" tasks take a lot more time than they actually do. Have your child time the task, and discuss the results.

3. **Set up a routine and stick with it.** Once your child understands how to meet your expectations and the time it is going to take to complete a task, use the external time tools described in chapter three: "Time Tools Are Critical." Your child is going to need external reminders to develop the habit. Timers, dry erase boards, and checklists made by drawing out the steps are all helpful.

4. **Start small and have patience.** Pick just one conflict to work on at a time. Remember, your child is going to need your support to practice this new routine over and over and over and over again before it will become automatic. Creating those brain pathways that bypass the weaknesses in the EF system takes time. Celebrate each day he gets it right, and don't lose it when he doesn't remember. Practice builds skills.

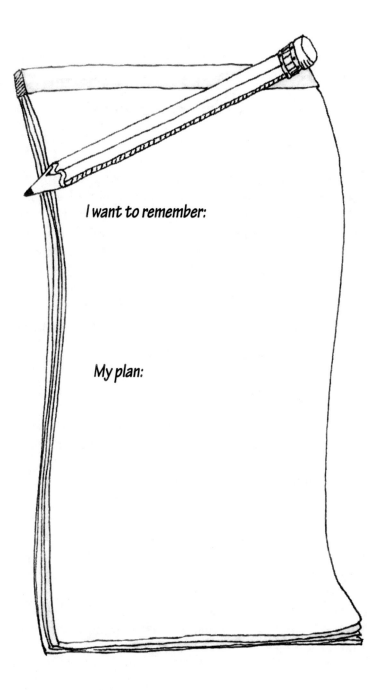

I want to remember:

My plan:

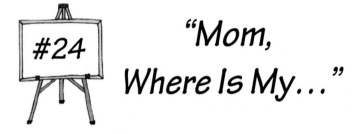

#24

"Mom, Where Is My..."

Children with executive function challenges commonly lose or misplace things. Because children with EF difficulties are living in the now, when they are finished with an object, they just mindlessly set it down wherever and move on. Misplaced cell phones, missing shoes, and school project directions that never make it home are all indications of a mind that, at a minimum, has issues with working memory (*I just set that down. Where did I put it?*), thinking ahead (*Where do I put this so that I can find it later?*), and organization (*Where does this belong?*).

Everything Needs a "Home"

There was a time in my life when I had five sets of keys. I'd leave them in pockets, on dressers, on tables, in purses and bags, etc. When it came to time to leave the house, I often couldn't find any of the keys! Of course that meant I was frantically running around hunting for them, which made me late for appointments.

I finally settled the problem when I decided enough already. I'd have one place for one set of keys, and I would always put them back in their designated "home" pocket in my purse. It took a little while to train my brain to put the keys in the purse pocket as soon as I unlocked the door. Now if I accidentally forget and set them on the kitchen counter with a bag of groceries, I will stop putting away the food and immediately return the keys to their pocket. That solved the problem of the missing keys. But my next problem was finding my purse. I solved that by creating a "home" for my purse: on the chair at the very top of the stairs. It goes there as soon as I enter the house. It's an easy place to see and to access.

Help Your Child Create Homes for Belongings

1. **Start with one object.** With your child, choose one object that is always disappearing and causes stress and conflicts for both of you.
2. **Keep it easy and in sight.** Choose a home location that is in sight and easy to access. The less travel time to get to an object's home, the better!
3. **Offer support and reminders.** Support your child's habit of returning that object to its home. In the beginning it is going to take effort on your part to do the reminding. The key here is to not just give your child a verbal reminder and assume she will do it. You must confirm that she actually walks the object to its home over and over again. It's this physical repetition of the action that will create the habit of putting that object away where she can find it.
4. **Create a home for another object.** Once your child is consistently putting away one object, you can go through this process again. Remember, it takes time to create behavior change. Little by little, your child will get better at putting away belongings so that they can be found quickly and easily.

If transporting papers to and from school is the problem, see tips #11 and #12.

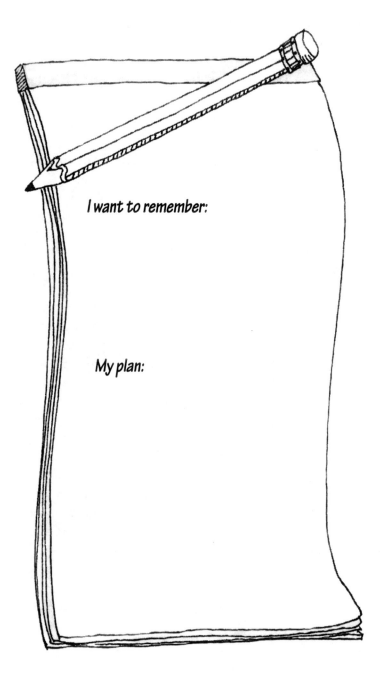

I want to remember:

My plan:

The Forgetful Child

Limited working memory is a huge problem for many children with EF challenges. Working memory limitations cause parents and teachers considerable frustrations because the "forgetful child" seems to just not care or not be paying attention. You end up constantly reminding him to do things, over and over and over...

During one session with me, the mother of a delightful, creative, and rather hyper sixth grader blurted out in frustration, "Why can't he ever remember to brush his hair? Every morning I have to send him back upstairs to brush his hair. He brushes his teeth. Why can't he remember to brush his hair?"

I turned to her son and asked, "Where do you keep your hairbrush?"

"In the drawer," he responded.

"Well," I replied, "that explains it. You just broke my first truth of time—out of sight out of mind." I could see the light bulbs go on in all of their faces. Because they were participating in my "Seeing My Time" course, they had learned about my first truth of time. They now understood the source of the problem. He didn't see the hairbrush, so he didn't think about brushing his hair.

Connect a New Habit to an Old Habit

I explained to this family that for years I had been unsuccessful at remembering to floss my teeth daily. Then it finally dawned on me that my floss was kept in a drawer—out of sight and thus out of mind! Once I moved the floss to sit right next to the toothpaste, I suddenly became remarkably consistent with flossing my teeth. I have created a new habit by piggybacking on an old, established habit—brushing my teeth before I go to bed.

To solve this family's hair-brushing issue, I suggested the hairbrush be kept directly next to the son's toothbrush or toothpaste. Having the hairbrush in plain sight as he brushed his teeth increased the odds of his remembering a task that doesn't have a lot of importance to this eleven-year-old male.

Three Steps to Help Alleviate Forgetfulness

1. **Keep a reminder of the task in sight.** This will provide a visual reminder of what your child needs to do.
2. **Create a new habit by linking it visually to an existing habit.**
3. **Use timers on phones or tablets to send reminders.** See tip #9 for more on timers.

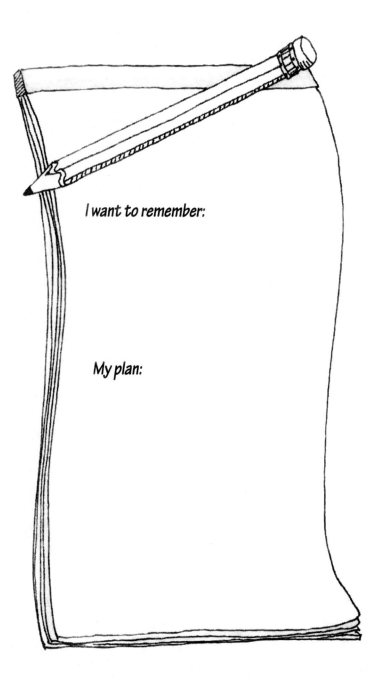

I want to remember:

My plan:

Starting Homework and Chores

Most students don't want to do homework or chores. This of course is very natural. Who wants to come home from a day of school, which is work for a student, only to do more work? Getting started, or task initiation, is another EF skill. It is especially hard to activate that part of the brain for something "I don't want to do."

I recently had an eighteen-year-old client a few weeks away from leaving for college. She acknowledged that she struggled with motivating herself to do things that she didn't want to do. Cleaning up her bedroom before leaving for college was becoming a big issue for her and her mother. After the session on using time tools to externally support a brain's EF weaknesses, she started to use a timer to motivate herself to get started. Setting it for just fifteen minutes, she promised herself that she would clean and when it went off, she could stop and do something that she wanted to do. She had a look of relief and a bit of amazement when she told me, "I've even started on the stuff under my bed." Little by little, the room was cleaned, and she was able to take off for college without that messy room hanging over her head, thus avoiding a renewed conflict when she returned home at Thanksgiving.

Use Timers for Motivation

A timer can give you that little push to get started. Sometimes you keep going after the timer goes off because you've got the time, the momentum, and the motivation to finish. However, if you work on a big task for even fifteen minutes, you've accomplished something! Celebrate what you have done and move on. You can schedule another fifteen minutes to work on it later. Over time you'll chip away at that "I don't want to do it" task and get it done.

Help Your Child to Get Started

1. **Set a goal.** Tell your child to decide how long he wants to work on a specific homework assignment or chore. Give him some choice; however, make the time long enough to be useful but short enough to be a goal that feels easily reachable. Fifteen minutes is a good minimum.
2. **Set a timer.** To work most effectively, work without distractions. Read chapter seven for tips on handling distractions.
3. **Reset the timer?** When the timer goes off, your child might find himself motivated to continue to finish the assignment, especially if the end is in sight.

 *Notepad*

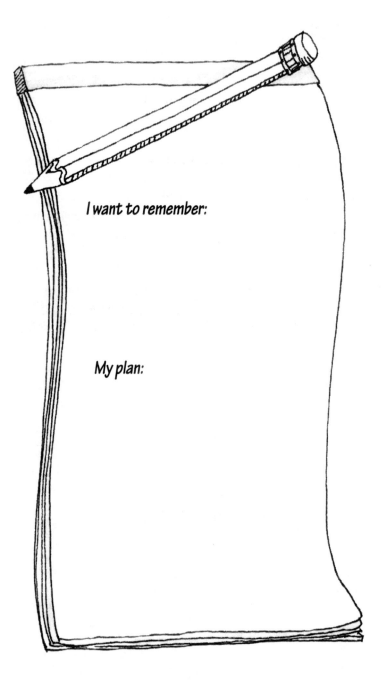

I want to remember:

My plan:

#27 *Stop Being Late*

To get out the door in time for school, work, appointments, etc., timers can be very helpful. My time-challenged brain lies to me. It tells me that it takes me three minutes to leave the house. Wrong. It can take me fifteen minutes. I know. I've timed it. As I am leaving, I've got to go to the bathroom, grab a coat, stick a couple of dishes in the dishwasher as I walk through the kitchen, and anything else that strikes me on my way out. Likewise, when you holler at a child, "It's time to go!" she will need to stop doing something and collect herself and her gear. This can take up a bit of time, more than you may have allowed. That leads to yelling and arriving late to school.

Set a timer to begin all transitions. Set it for fifteen minutes *before* you need to leave, but *start* leaving when it goes off.

 Notepad

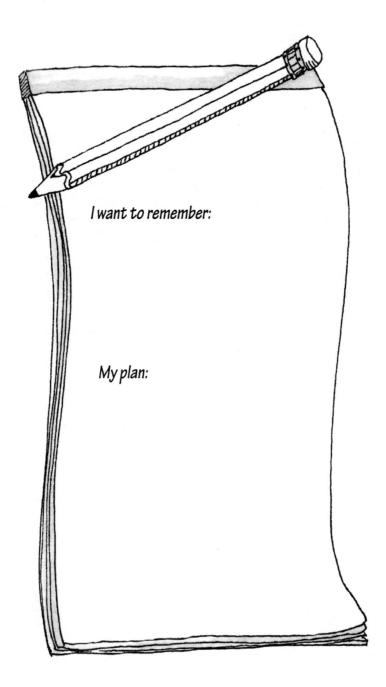

I want to remember:

My plan:

Interrupting Hyper-Focus

Some children get into an activity and don't want to stop, even though they need to move on to accomplish other necessary tasks. This can happen to me when I step into my yard to start trimming and weeding. I'll just keep going and going, neglecting other things that I had on my to-do list. Students can do this too, sometimes hyper-focusing on things you wish they wouldn't—video games or creating a "perfect" illustration for a report—when they haven't done the more demanding writing for the report.

Annoying Timers Break Hyper-Focus

I recommend a digital timer that has an incessant, annoying beep. This kind of timer penetrates a hyper-focusing brain, creating a pause point to remember why the timer is going off. When I go out to weed in my yard, I wear my timer that goes around my neck. When it goes off, I know that it is time to stop, *now*, not after I pull just one more weed.

 *Notepad*

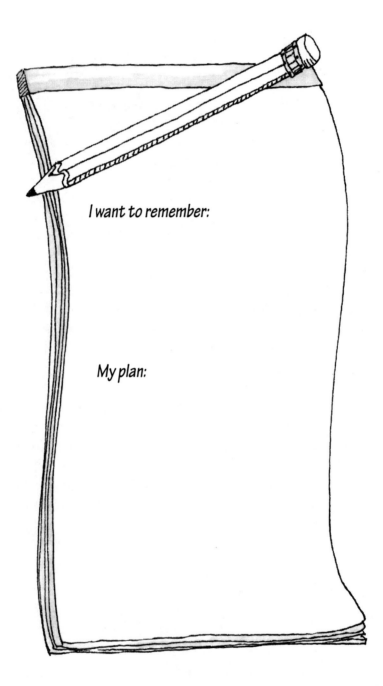

I want to remember:

My plan:

Music and Studying

#29

A lot of parents voice their frustration with their children listening to music while they study. Usually it is the type of music that is the bone of contention. Not all types of music support the brain while doing homework. To complicate matters, I'm hearing different opinions from the research world on this issue. So here's what I'm telling parents these days:

1. **Some research supports music being useful for students who have ADHD.** It appears to help them focus on homework. That makes a bit of sense to me, because some ADHD folks seem to be hypersensitive to random sounds, which they find distracting. For these people, calm instrumental music can act as a cover for other noises, making focus easier.
2. **Avoid music with lyrics.** Our brains are wired to pay attention to language. The brain doesn't multi-task, so a phrase in a song can easily be distracting, pulling a person's mind away from a task. It happens to me all the time. I now only listen to songs with lyrics when I'm doing something mindless, like cleaning.
3. **If you are a trained musician or singer, study in quiet.** I base this statement on my musically inclined clients, who report getting lost in all types of music because they are able to analyze the composition and structure of the piece. I can't do that, so Mozart works great for me as background music.

4. **Set up a playlist appropriate for studying.** Many students have elaborate collections of digital music and get distracted stopping to choose the next song. On a Saturday or during the summer, have your child create the perfect nonvocal playlist for studying.

5. **Consider the value of silence.** Some researchers today are discussing their concerns that our noisy, overstimulating environments are damaging our long-term brain health. Quiet is easier on our brains. Just as it takes energy to focus, our brains use energy to shut out distractions. While writing the last parts of this book, I decided to not listen to any kind of music to see if silence made it easier to focus on my writing. I discovered that I was more productive in silence.

Is Music Worth a Battle?

If your child is getting his homework done in a reasonable time and turning out quality work, then let go of your issue. If he isn't, you might want to have your child conduct some experiments, timing how long homework takes with music or without. What type of music made homework easier? What type of music was distracting and got in the way of homework?

You may need to do some negotiations on this issue. Is this a battle that needs fighting or is worth fighting?

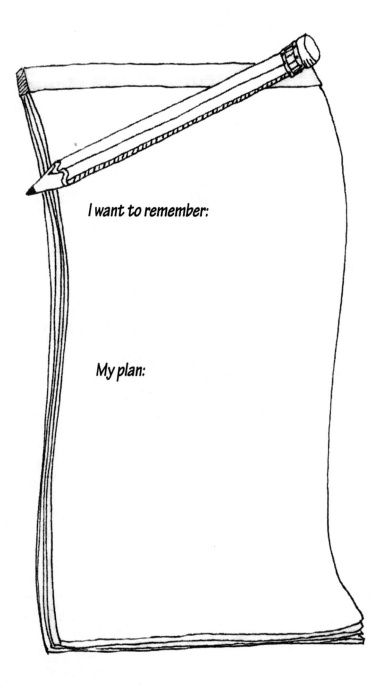

I want to remember:

My plan:

seven

Handling Distractions

I've heard it said that if you weren't born with attention deficit disorder, you would end up acquiring it simply because of all the distractions that bombard us in our daily lives. Smartphones, tablets, and computers bring an entire planet's worth of distracting information to our attention, whether we want it or not. It can all be overwhelming, and it is really distracting if you're trying to accomplish anything. Even a brain with naturally good focus and impulse control succumbs to other aspects of our brain's wiring: our natural curiosity to learn (reading random articles on the web and watching YouTube videos) and a drive for connection to others (Facebook, LinkedIn, Twitter, etc.). These brain traits suck us into the abyss of distractions before we know it.

A child with EF challenges doesn't stand much of a chance at self-control with all the temptations at her fingertips. Your child is going to need your help and your support to learn to say no to distractions. The tips in this chapter offer suggestions to handle the most common sources of distraction for your child.

The Lie of Multitasking

We have so many expectations and demands placed on our limited time that multitasking seems to be the only way to survive. However, research is informing us that constantly dividing our attention isn't good for our brain health or for our ability to efficiently get things done.

Multitasking is a huge problem for children and adolescents with EF challenges. I asked a nineteen-year-old what he did while doing his homework. Here was his list:

1. Play video games with friends
2. Fill out applications for work
3. Answer emails
4. Surf the web and read items of interest
5. Read and write comments on social networks
6. Pick out and evaluate new songs for a playlist
7. Eat
8. Respond to texts
9. Homework

The Brain Isn't Designed to Multitask

Science has proved that the conscious human brain does one thing at a time. Every time we shift focus, the brain must stop. It has to access information about the new task before it can refocus and move forward on that new task. All of that shifting back and forth is very inefficient. It depletes valuable brain energy—think about tired children at the end of a school day. When you multitask, the rate of errors increases, which results in things like increased errors on math homework. And it wastes valuable time. The effect of all this multitasking stresses the brain. I've even heard some people say that multitasking makes you dumber. While I'm not sure about that, I am sure that multitasking does not make you smarter.

To Stop Multitasking, Stop Multitasking

In the following pages are tips to handle some of the common distractions that have a negative impact on your child's success at school and at home. I encourage you to consider other ways to limit distractions around your home.

 *Notepad*

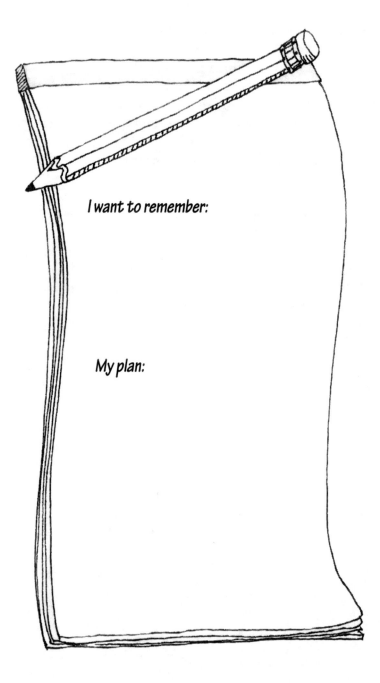

I want to remember:

My plan:

Managing Screen Devices

#31

Screens are everywhere, and they wreak havoc on our ability to get things done. The games, the apps, the texting, the instant access to emails, the internet marketing—all are very carefully designed to keep us connected to these distractions. Don't get me wrong, I have my fair share of devices. And I won't go on a rant about how using them is changing the wiring in our brains in ways we don't yet fully understand. Instead, I want to advise you to limit access to screens to promote your child's development of his executive function skills and his time management. Have the confidence to set ground rules. Children with EF challenges have difficulty with self-regulation, or controlling their own behavior. They often simply can't say no to the temptations of technology.

It Is Okay to Set Limits

Despite the protests of children, there is life and fun to be had with friends without constant video game playing or texting. Many parents of successful children set boundaries. Yes, some go so far as to say no to video games during the school week. Their kids thrive doing quality homework and hanging out in person with friends. The key is limiting access to the temptations. This means you may need to do the following:

1. **No TV or personal computers in bedrooms.** Distractions in a bedroom not only get in the way of homework, but they can also get in the way of getting adequate sleep. Many a child fakes being asleep when you check on them. If you are concerned about your child's sleep, see tip #44.

2. **Collect all game devices and store them until homework and chores are completed.** You might want to collect these before bedtime too so sleep isn't disrupted.

3. **Collect smartphones, tablets, and laptops at bedtime.** Recharge them in your bedroom, not your child's. For more about managing phones, see tips #32 and #33.

4. **Set limits for the amount of time your child can be on screens.** You may need to negotiate this depending on her age. You just want to be sure she is getting quality work and chores done before play. Stick with your limits!

5. **No screens at the dinner table.** Talking to people is good for the development of social skills, empathy, and the ability to read all-important nonverbal communication from people's faces and body language. Texting doesn't develop these critical neuron networks in the brain.

6. **Install internet blocking software.** One option for computers is Freedom, found at macfreedom.com. There is also a Freedom app for cell phones and iPads. This product allows students to block themselves from the internet for a specified time while using the computer applications needed for homework, such as word processing. My daughter chose this route when she wasn't focusing on getting her senior thesis work done because she was always checking the internet news. You can investigate other blocking software options, including one offered by Google.

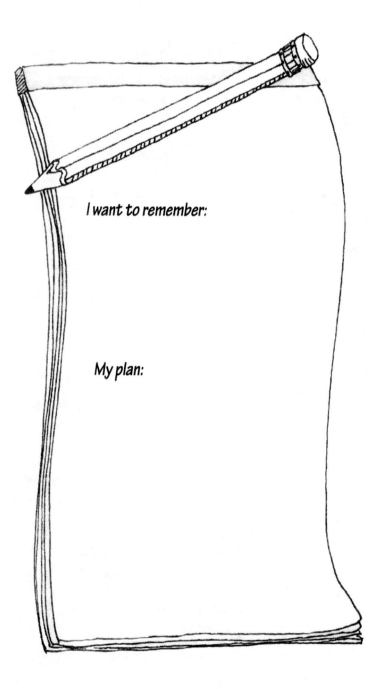

I want to remember:

My plan:

Cell Phones and Homework

Staying connected to friends is critical for the adolescent crowd, so many teens do homework with their phones close at hand. There is a lot of social pressure to instantly respond to text messages.

All that shifting between texting and homework does two things: it makes homework take longer, and each shift in focus increases the rate of errors on the homework assignment.

No Phones During Homework

To prevent a potential outburst of anger from your child, frame limiting access to the phone during homework as being supportive of your child's success, not as a punishment. I was thrilled when a sophomore student who was determined to do better in school than he had as a freshman told me his plan to put all of his electronic devices in a container when he gets home from school. He told me he was going to turn them over to Mom so he could avoid temptations. Now, that was an example of some pretty grown-up metacogniton! To build evidence that homework sessions will go faster without the phone, follow the advice in tip #18 and time homework with distractions and again without distractions.

Inform the Friends

I suggest that students text friends or post on their social media network that they will be offline for the next hour or so doing homework. Announce a time to reconnect. That way your student can focus on work and make sure that his friends are clear that they are not being ignored.

If your child easily slips into the distractions on his phone, ask if you can help him stay on task by monitoring the phone in another room for him. Please note: It may be the case that your child needs to text a friend about a homework assignment. If he needs help from a classmate, he can come and ask you for the phone.

 *Notepad*

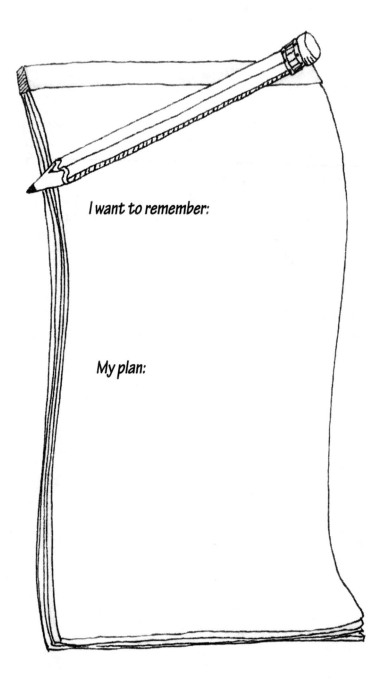

I want to remember:

My plan:

Screens and Sleepy Teens

#33

Is your child dragging in the morning despite turning the lights out at a reasonable time? You may need to take ownership of your child's phone at night. A physician who specializes in sleep issues explained to me that a large percentage of children and adolescents are going to bed with their phones, and they are awakened during the night (sometimes multiple times) by friends texting them.

The Connection Between Sleep and Grades

These nocturnal interruptions have negative impacts on the executive functions of adolescents. They need nine hours of good sleep to function at their best during school. For effective learning, a student needs to go through several uninterrupted sleep cycles each night, during which the brain solidifies the learning of the previous day. Grades go down when quality sleep goes down.

Are Night Calls and Texts a Problem?

Before removing the phone, make sure this really is a problem by talking with your child and checking phone use records. If you do decide it is best to keep the phone out of her room at night (currently recommended by the American Academy of Pediatrics), be sure to let her contact friends and let them know that she will no longer be able to respond to nighttime contacts after *your* bedtime. This situation calls for tough love. Your child may not be able to place limits on either her own or her friends' behaviors. Some phone services provide another option where you can block texts and calls after a certain hour.

By having your child's phone at night, you can charge it in your room and hand it back to her in the morning. This has the additional benefit of your child having a charged phone when you want to reach her!

Other Reasons for Poor Sleep

Late-night phone use isn't the only reason your child might be sleepy in the morning. Tip #44 has more about screens and sleep. If your child seems tired all the time, a good book to read is *Snooze or Lose*, by Dr. Helene Emsellem, in addition to the information later in this book.

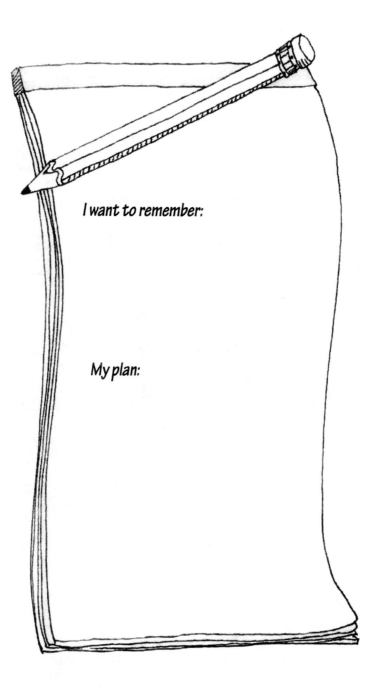

I want to remember:

My plan:

eight

Challenging Chores

I am rather concerned at how few of my student clients have regular chores to do around their homes. Many report having no chores or that they sometimes help with dishes or take out the trash once a week. Some report that they have to clean their rooms. However, by the glances that are shared between parent and child after this pronouncement, I doubt cleaning the room is really happening on a regular basis.

I'm concerned because learning to do chores independently is critical brain training for adulthood. In essence, doing chores is the foundation of building a work ethic. Transitioning into the demands of the adult work world or adult relationships requires more than being able to do homework and play on a sports team. Too many adolescents leave home with no life skills for independent living: cooking, cleaning, and managing money.

Research Supports Chores

This isn't just me ranting. There is research to back up the value of chores. A University of Minnesota study found that the regular completion of chores around the home was a strong indicator for success as an adult.

This makes sense from the perspective of the brain and executive functions. A primary role of executive functions is to self-regulate or to control one's behavior in order to get things done. Completing chores requires the development and use of multiple executive function skills:

- **Delaying gratification:** doing work before play
- **Planning, prioritizing, and problem solving:** completing chores that have multiple steps and unforeseen challenges
- **Focus and goal-directed behavior:** sticking with a chore until it is properly done
- **Time management:** fitting chores in and around school responsibilities and fun activities

Putting in the time to help your child develop the habit of doing a chore well and on time is a vital role for parents, especially for those who have children with significant executive function challenges. Set up clear expectations for help around the house. Carefully teach them how to do the task. Have age-appropriate expectations (tip #34 has a list by age). Be consistent. Be strong. Be determined. Doing chores is for their own good!

In this chapter you'll find a detailed way to teach your child to do a multistep chore and address the common complaints about unkempt bedrooms, plus thoughts on motivation.

"That Is Not a Clean Room"

#34

A common complaint from parents is that they just get tired of nagging their children to do chores. When my kids were little, I couldn't figure out how to motivate my children to consistently do chores *and* to do them to meet my standards. (My own time-challenged behavior didn't help the situation.) I know now that the problem was centered in my not understanding their brain development (or my own) and not properly teaching them to do multistep tasks.

Completing Chores Requires Good Executive Skills

Just like homework, chores require good executive functioning skills. You have to plan ahead, break tasks into steps, and have goal-directed persistence—sticking with it until you get the chore done.

How do you teach your kids to do chores so that you don't have to remind them all the time? Follow the adage "little by little."

As I was thinking about writing this section about chores, I read a book by Richard Lavoie, *The Motivation Breakthrough.* His method of teaching a multistep task makes great sense from the point of view of the brain and learning. While Lavoie was specifically addressing how to teach a child who suffers from learned helplessness, I think his steps can help everyone learn how to do multiple-step tasks. I've adapted his ideas a bit to include building your child's connection between a chore and the amount of time it actually takes.

Pick One Task You Want Done

Pick a task or skill you want your child to learn to do independently. Start with just one, and make it developmentally appropriate. And don't be afraid to start young! Here are some guidelines suggested by Richard Lavoie:

- **2 to 4 years:** pick up toys and clothes—10 minutes daily
- **5 to 7 years:** feed animals, dust, pick up clothes, care for plants—10 to 15 minutes daily
- **8 to 12 years:** vacuum, make your own lunch, clear the table, load the dishwasher, take out the recycling and garbage, do simple food prep, put clean laundry into drawers—15 to 20 minutes daily
- **12+ years:** prepare family meals, wash the car, do yard work, do laundry, shop, and run errands—20 to 30 minutes daily.

Teach How to Do a Task Correctly

This will take an investment of some time and focus on your part, but it will pay off big once your child has the task down and can do it independently. No more nagging!

The key is to break the task into smaller chunks. Cleaning the bathroom might first start with just cleaning the toilet. Let your child master that before moving on. Cleaning the whole bedroom can be daunting, so start with making the bed or picking up the floor.

1. **Do it for your child.** Yes, you read that correctly—
   you have to do the chore in order to model exactly
   how you want the task done. It is very important
   to talk aloud as you do it and explain the steps as
   you go. This modeling and explaining develops your
   child's metacognition connected to doing the task
   "the right way."

   - **Record the time.** I recommend that you make
     your child the time keeper as you teach the task.
     Have her record exactly how long it takes to com-
     plete the chore, start to finish. Often when we
     have something "not fun" to do, our brain imag-
     ines that it is going to take a lot of time to com-
     plete, so we put it off and put it off. People are
     often amazed at how little time it actually takes to
     do a chore. Collecting data on how long it really
     takes to finish something is a very important part
     of developing time management and getting past
     procrastination.

   - **Model the chore repeatedly.** Continue to do
     the chore, while your child watches and records
     your actions, over several days. The number of
     times you have to model the chore will depend
     upon your child's executive functioning develop-
     ment. Don't stop at just a couple of times, espe-
     cially if this is a task that is done weekly rath-
     er than daily. It takes time to get multiple-step
     tasks into long-term memory. After a couple of
     sessions, ask your child to tell you the next step
     that *you* need to do. Lavoie says of this step, "Do
     not require him to physically participate or assist
     during step one." That advice is going to take
     patience on your part!

2. **Do the chore with your child.** At this point, gradually include the child in the process. Give him a step

to do, and then you do the rest. As you continue with step two, he goes from helping you with the chore to the point where you are helping him with the chore. At the end of this step, your child should be completing the task independently. *Don't stop here!*

3. **Watch your child do the chore.** This is a critical step I would never have figured out on my own. Lavoie says if you leave it out, you've been wasting your time—you won't get the child to independence. Once your child has mastered step two, have her call you when she begins to do the task on her own. You are now the observer and the time recorder. Offer suggestions. Give honest praise and reinforcement: "You did that quickly and easily." "That was very well done." "It must feel good to do such a good job." "I really appreciate your help." "With your work done, you can now do what you want."

4. **Take a picture.** You might want your child to record his "independently well-done chore" with a photograph. This would work for the well-made bed, the cleared-off desk, the first muffins baked, or the first pasta sauce made from scratch. The photos can be shared with Grandma or Facebook, or put on the refrigerator. The photo can also be used the next time the chore needs doing. Hand it to him, and tell him to match his picture. When he has matched the picture, he can mark the task off his whiteboard. Once you are convinced that he has truly mastered the task, then it is time for step five.

5. **Have your child do the chore.** Don't slip and take over the job once she has mastered it. Have that chore become a permanent and consistent part of her day or week plan, which is kept in sight on a personal whiteboard or on a family whiteboard. It is part of her job to mark it off as finished so you can see that it is done without asking. Read tip #7 about how to create a family whiteboard.

Summary of the Steps for Independent Chores

1. **Do it for your child,** talking as you go.
2. **Do it with your child,** asking questions as you go.
3. **Watch your child do it,** encouraging and reminding.
4. **Let your child do it,** allowing her to cross it off her list.

When choosing a chore to begin this process, pick a chore that is really important for your child to master. Pay attention to your child's age, and choose something that is not too complicated, with too many steps. "Clean your bedroom," is daunting for many children and adolescents, especially if the room is out of control. The next three tips, numbers 35–37, address how to approach the "disaster bedroom."

To ensure the job isn't accidentally "forgotten," you might make the chore semi-permanent on the family whiteboard by using removable labels. Write the task on the label, and position it in the child's section of the board. When he finishes the task, rather than drawing a line through it, he would just put a check mark next to it when he is done.

 *Notepad*

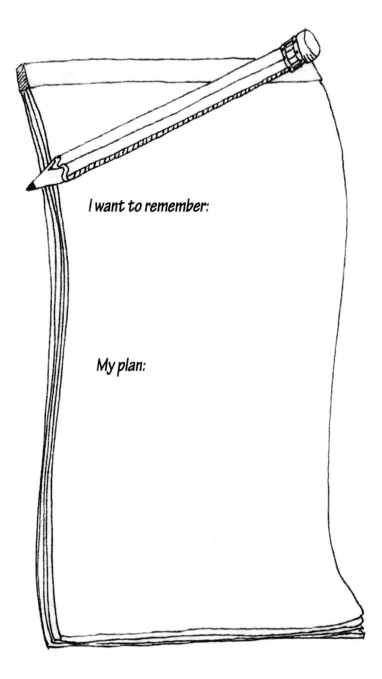

I want to remember:

My plan:

#35   *The Disaster Bedroom—Part I*

Messy rooms drive some parents nuts. Conflicts often occur when the request to "clean your room" isn't done to the level of the parent's expectations.

Once again I want you to pause and get inside the mind of the child with executive function challenges, this time as she walks into a room to clean it. First, she crashes into task initiation challenges—*Where do I start?!* She can get paralyzed right there. Challenges with sustained focus abound as she gets distracted by what she is supposed to be putting away. If your child has a brain that struggles with organization, she can't figure out where to put something, so it all gets shoved to the bottom of a closet or drawer. And finally, cleaning a whole messy room can be overwhelming, so she gives up, a victim of her brain's inability to have goal-directed persistence. You will need to approach the messy room in steps, and provide support as the room gets under control.

Analyze the Problem

Walk into your child's room and ask yourself two questions:

1. Is there too much "stuff" in this room?
2. Does every object in this room have a home where it belongs?

We will begin with question one. The second question we will address in our next tip, #36.

Get Rid of Things!

In our modern consumer culture, it is really easy to accumulate stuff. As a result, it doesn't take long for any organized space to become overwhelmed by new belongings. Create space and order by getting rid of things.

Set a timer for thirty minutes. Along with your child, start in one area of the room. Pick up objects to determine if they "stay" or "go." Look at each object and ask if it is really important now in your child's life. If not, look at the object and say, "It is time for you to become someone else's treasure." Then, pop it into a bag for Goodwill or another organization that accepts donations.

If something has sentimental attachment but you don't want it taking up space in your home anymore, take a picture of it so you can store the memory of the object digitally. Your child could take these pictures and create a digital memories album.

Plan on Helping

This sorting process is emotionally draining with lots of decisions to make, so I advise you help your child with it. Older teens may simply need your help to get started. When my daughter felt overwhelmed by starting a big room-cleaning session, she would often ask me for help. I would show up with a couple of bags and help for a few minutes until she could keep at it on her own.

Attack the Disaster Room in Chunks

When the timer goes off after thirty minutes, determine if there is time and energy to continue on for another thirty minutes. If not, carry the "toss" bag to your car so you are reminded to drop it off at a donation site. Celebrate the progress with your child. Then schedule a date to sort through another section of the room. Little by little, the room will feel better to both you and your child.

Once you've done all of the sorting, you'll be ready for the second step of ending a disaster bedroom described in the next tip, #36.

 **Notepad**

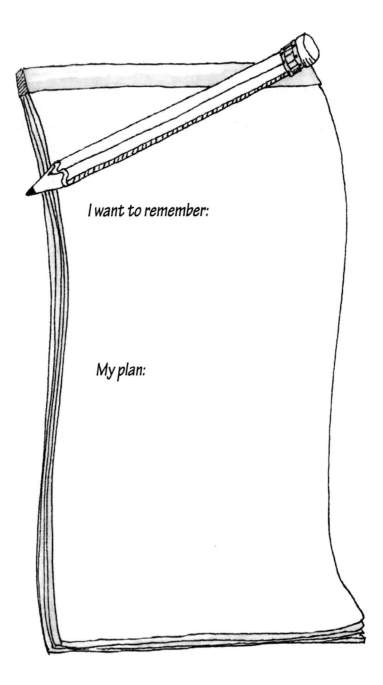

I want to remember:

My plan:

#36 The Disaster Bedroom—Part II

The first step to making it easier to clean a room is to sort through all of those belongings to determine if they *currently* have significant value for your child. The previous tip guides you through the process where we asked the question: Is there too much stuff in this room?

Once you have a room that is full of only "keep" items and the "toss" items have been donated, you are ready to answer the second question: Does every object in this room have a home where it belongs?

"A place for everything and everything in its place" is a very valuable concept to instill in your child. With this understanding embedded in the brain, cleaning up goes much faster, and organized rooms are easier to maintain.

Survey the "Homeless" Objects

1. **Make a list.** What categories of things are currently in piles?
2. **What kind of home is needed?** For each object or category of objects, decide how you might create a home. For example:
   - Does the room need more bookshelves or shelf space?

- Would labeled clear plastic containers be appropriate so you can see the contents easily and remember what is in the container?
- Are there places to put those containers so that they could be easily accessible?
- Would hooks for jackets, backpacks, and sports apparel be helpful?
- Is there a dirty clothes hamper without a lid so that it is easy to toss in clothes?
- Would a closet organization system make better use of valuable space? Would it provide home shelves for things beyond clothes and shoes?

3. **Get out a measuring tape:** Measure the room's wall space, closets, desktops, etc. (This is great to do with your child. Have him measure or record. This is math in real life.) Then take your list and go shopping! There are lots of stores that specialize in containers and closet organizers. Including your child in the shopping will help him engage in the process and invest in maintaining his organized room.

4. **Put things into their new home.** Once you've got your homes for things, set that timer again and spend some time with your child putting things away where they now belong. Your child may enjoy creating the labels for containers. Let her help in the decision-making process. If you can't get the room all set up in one time period, be sure to put a date on your calendar to complete the project.

If simply reading these tips for disaster rooms overwhelmed you and your brain, get help. Do you have a friend who would help you? Does your child have a friend who loves to organize? You can also hire a professional organizer.

Once you've got your child's room thinned out and organized, the final step is maintenance, described in the next tip, #37.

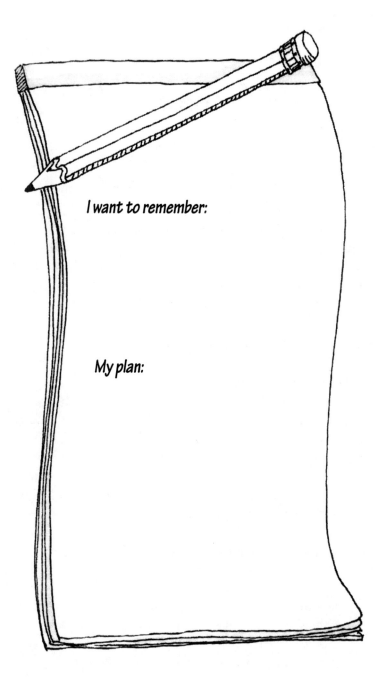

I want to remember:

My plan:

#37 The Disaster Bedroom—Part III

Once you have followed the previous two tips on handling disaster bedrooms, you are ready for maintenance. The bedroom should now be in a condition that allows your child to tidy it up without too much time and effort. That said, a child with EF challenges is still going to need assistance to develop the maintenance habit of cleaning her room.

Teach How to Clean a Room

Please remember that it takes repetition, repetition, and more repetition to create a habit. If a child's clean bedroom is critical in your world, you will need to be involved at the beginning for a chunk of time. Please refer back to tip #34 for a detailed description of the way to teach multistep tasks. The age of your child will have to be taken into consideration. Like many things, it is easier to start good cleaning habits when children are younger!

Steps to Support Maintaining a Tidy Room

1. **Model steps and record time.** Help your child tidy his room, modeling putting things back in their homes. Have him time how long it takes to do it. Discuss the time. Maintenance takes a lot less time than getting a disaster room under control!

2. **Schedule room cleaning.** Have your child always put "clean room" on her daily or weekend plan. Have her include the time it is going to take her.

3. **Take pictures.** Consider taking pictures of what a clean room looks like so that your expectations are clear. For example, take pictures of the clean desk, the clean floor, the made bed, the clothes put away. Show the pictures to your child and tell him that he is done with the chore when the room or area you've asked to have cleaned matches the picture.

4. **Help her get started.** For many children with EF deficits, marshaling the brain energy to start a cleaning project (or anything they don't want to do) is really hard. Rather than get angry and frustrated, it might be best if you help her get started. Then set a timer and leave, explaining you've got your own cleaning task to do. Perhaps you can race to see who gets done first.

Pick Your Battles

When my children were young, I didn't have the self-awareness and understanding of my own EF deficits to be able to properly support my children's room maintenance habits. While I now know the value of developing good cleaning habits, at the time I decided that battling over bedrooms just wasn't worth a fight. I saved my energy for bigger issues. What was my solution to their disaster bedrooms? I just closed their bedroom doors. If I couldn't see the mess, it didn't bother me! They have both managed to grow into reasonably organized adults capable of cleaning up after themselves. When my now-adult daughter read the draft of this section, she wrote me, "You saved yourself so much pain by not making me clean my room. I think it was a wise choice."

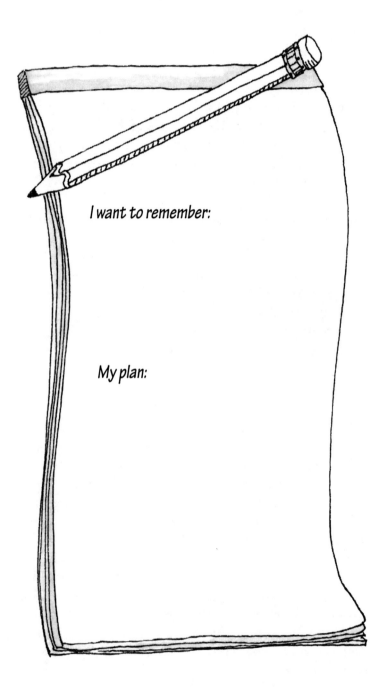

I want to remember:

My plan:

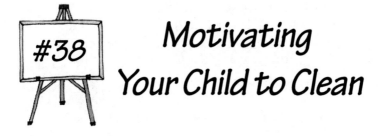

#38 Motivating Your Child to Clean

Motivating a child—or anyone—to do something he dosen't want to do is a challenge. Neither carrots nor sticks work for any length of time. Ultimately, motivation has to come from within. It often boils down to connecting to "What's in it for me?" This is rather self-centered, and it's hard for a child to connect a benefit for herself with completing a chore you've asked her to do. I suggest focusing on chores as being a component of being a family member. Chores are just part of life. Family members all do their share to make life work for everyone.

Use Technology to Motivate

While many experts tout using charts, checklists, and reward stickers to motivate children, I recently read an article with suggestions that sound more effective.

It turns out that enterprising software engineers—most likely parents themselves—have been creating apps that motivate children to do chores by offering incentives and points, much like video games. The apps I read about were designed with the under-twelve child in mind. Apparently siblings are racing to get through their chores so that they can beat each other!

By the time you read this, I'm sure there will be multiple

digital apps connected to motivating children to do chores. I encourage you to investigate the current options. In the meantime, here are some suggestions from the article I found in the *Wall Street Journal*, "Children Who Happily Do Chores, No Nagging Required."

- **You Rule Chores** works on smartphones.
- **Chore Monster** works on the web and on Apple devices.
- **RewardChart and Chore Pad** replaces traditional chore charts with their stickers and stars.

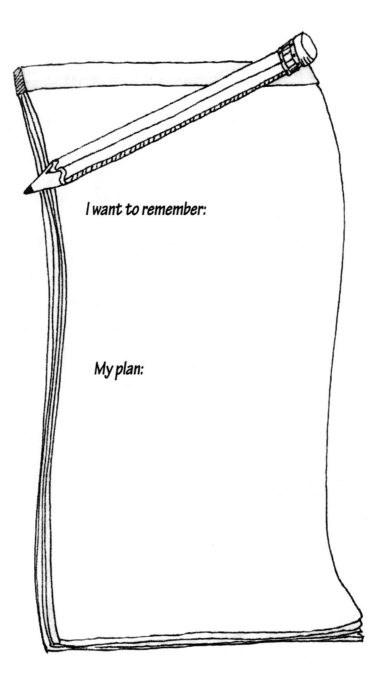

I want to remember:

My plan:

nine

Other Reasons Children Struggle in School

While EF challenges play a huge role in preventing a child from meeting the expectations of parents and teachers, they may not be the only stumbling blocks for your child's success. A child's behavior is a response to a tangle of genetics, brain development, and reactions to the environment around him. It can be a real puzzle to figure out what is behind your child's inability to get things done at school and at home.

Listen to your gut feelings. If you feel there is more than executive function deficits behind your child's struggles, please have the courage to seek help. Trust me, early intervention is better than late.

The tips in the preceding chapters of this book offered concrete ideas for supporting weaknesses in your child's executive skills. This chapter addresses other issues that you may need to investigate in order to fully understand the reasons behind your child's struggles.

How Are Your EF Skills?

When I work with families, it is very common for at least one parent to also have executive function challenges. As the old saying goes, an apple doesn't fall far from the tree. It's genetics in action.

If you are struggling with time management, planning, and organization, you may lack the skills to set up the home environment to support your child. Don't blame yourself. Be honest about having a problem and have the courage to get help. I was once in those shoes.

In the years prior to my oldest entering fourth grade, I was close to a disaster. My poor EF skills were having a negative impact on the entire family. I would yell at the kids in the morning because they (meaning we) were going to be late for school—again. They wouldn't have clean soccer clothes when they needed them. There wouldn't be food in the refrigerator for sack lunches. I was unable to set up routines for myself, much less routines to support them in completing homework and chores. You don't have to live like I did. Change is possible. The first step is to get some help.

Help Comes in Many Forms

1. **Read the tips in this book and apply them to your life.** This will be a positive change for your children. You can work together to improve in getting

things done by using external time tools and strategies. Start small with one or two of the tips, and then add another tip as you adjust. Little by little, change happens.

2. **Read more books about executive functioning.** In the resources list in the appendix, there is a list of books available at the time of this printing. More titles seem to be showing up daily, so search the web with the key words *executive functions*.

3. **Take a course on developing executive function skills.** Check out my website to learn about the "Seeing My Time" course for adults and families. It is designed to carefully support the whole family as it builds each member's self-awareness and EF skills toward getting things done. For information about how to participate in a course, visit us at www.Executive FunctioningSuccess.com.

4. **Hire a personal coach who has knowledge about executive functions.** Coaches who are trained to work with those who have ADHD would be a good place to start.

5. **Become a member of CHADD,** Children and Adults with Attention-Deficit/Hyperactivity Disorder. They have an excellent website, informative email newsletters, and their *Attention* magazine often has articles on the topic of executive functions for adults. Some communities have a CHADD support group. They also have online courses for parents at www. CHADD.org.

 *Notepad*

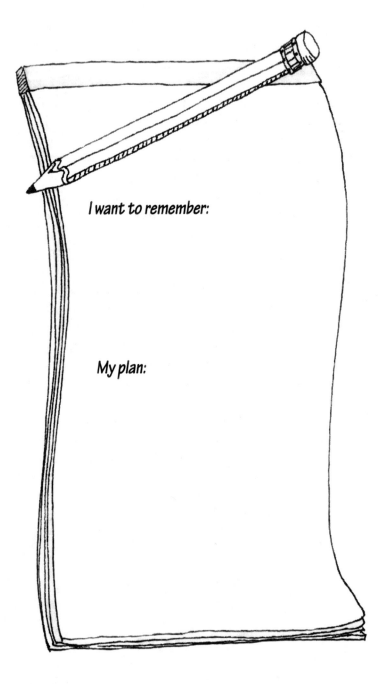

I want to remember:

My plan:

Is the School the Best Match?

If your child is struggling in school, he is at risk for developing a mindset of being a failure. You might want to take a second look at the school environment. Over the years I've seen well-intentioned parents who are determined to keep their child in a school setting that is simply not a match for that child's needs. This can even happen in certain types of private schools that, because of their child development philosophy, lack the awareness or skills to support children who have learning disabilities or executive function deficits.

Some alternative schools do have wonderful programs. But they may also have limitations that are not obvious at first glance. If your child needs services or supports that are not a part of that school's structure, your child will not ultimately become the learner either you or the school dream about producing. This is especially true if your child is struggling with or avoiding learning to read or has significant executive function deficits. Tip #41 talks more about learning disabilities.

Explore Your School Options

Today in many communities, there are private and public school options. Here's what to look for:

1. **A good fit:** You want a match for your child's brain *and* personality.

2. **A positive environment:** You want an encouraging, supportive environment in which your child feels safe asking questions when she's confused.

3. **EF suppports:** You want structures in place and teachers who support the growth of your child's executive skills so that he will transition as smoothly as possible through the increasing demands of school.

4. **Services for learning differences:** You want a school that supports learning differences, including dyslexia.

5. **Fosters active learning:** And of course you want stimulating and challenging academic opportunities that engage your child. You want an educational setting that prepares your child to become a lifelong learner, which is what is needed to be successful in this rapidly changing work world.

You Are the Buyer of Services

If your community has choices and your child is starting to succumb to failure, spend time checking out the educational options in your community.

1. **Visit different schools.** Interview the school leaders and ask about their philosophy for dealing with children who have executive functioning deficits. What kind of support do classroom teachers offer? Has their staff training been connected to executive functions?

2. **Talk to parents of the school's students.** Ask to attend a parent meeting to get a feel for the types of families who attend the school. Interview some parents about their experiences and ask if any of them have children who have struggled in school.

3. **Find out if the school curriculum supports children with dyslexia.** If your child has had any challenges with learning to read, he is going to need help and

accommodations. Beware of an educator who tells you that there is no such thing as dyslexia. She is behind the times and the research.

4. **Not every school fits every child.** Don't assume that a school that was a perfect fit for your first child will be a perfect fit for your second child.

5. **Have your child visit the schools.** Have your child spend a day visiting schools that you are strongly considering. Honor his feelings about the school. A school that you would have loved to attend might not be the best match for your child.

What If I Don't Have Any Private School Options?

Don't give up if your only option is a local public school—which can be very good, by the way. Some districts have charter schools designed to work with different kinds of learners. Work within the system to set up positive relationships with the administration and teachers. You may need to be an educator yourself by providing the principal or teacher with a book on executive functions. Book titles for teachers are listed in the resources section of the appendix. Perhaps the school could use professional development on executive functions. Check out my website for our school offerings: www.ExecutiveFunctioning Success.com.

Homeschooling

If you can't find a school option to meet your child's needs, you might consider homeschooling. Today there are homeschooling networks and support groups. There are online schools and prepared curriculum. Check with your state's department of education for guidelines.

Homeschooling is not for every family. It requires a parent with the time and the skills to provide the necessary daily structure for a learning environment. It requires a good working relationship between the parent and the child. Be honest with yourself about your own schedule and skills before going down this path.

Three Things to Do While Investigating Schools

1. **Keep educating yourself.** Learn more about your child's strengths and weaknesses from a brain perspective by reading "Evaluating Executive Function Skills" in the appendix. Read more about executive functions in books listed in the resources section of the appendix.
2. **Get help.** Find professionals to support your child's weaknesses. See tip#41.
3. **Support your child.** Do your very best to support your child at home to get things done for school. Use the tips in chapter four.

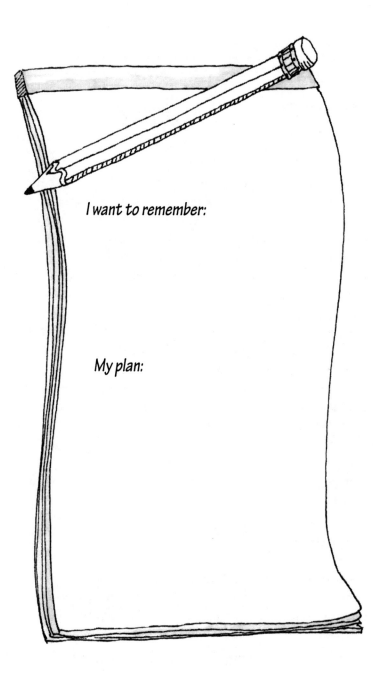

I want to remember:

My plan:

Learning Differences

As I stated at the beginning of this chapter, deficits in executive functions are not the only reason a student struggles to get schoolwork done. I will never forget a family session when a mother—a special education teacher herself—excitedly sat down with her ninth grader, who had significant dyslexia. The three of us had been meeting for a few weeks at this point. At the beginning of sessions, I always ask participants about what has been working well. This day, Mom looked at me and crowed, "Last night he just sat down and did his homework. No delaying. No complaining. He just did it!" Then she turned to him, eyes still shining, "I didn't want to interrupt you last night, but tell me, what strategies did you use? What were you thinking? How did you do it?"

He looked at her and said, "I could." The mom and I paused to let the significance of that answer sink in. He continued, "I did it because I could do it. I understood how to do it."

You Can't Do What You Can't Do

That young man was coming home with homework that he either lacked the knowledge to do, or he was unable to read his assignment well enough to do it. He was being labeled "difficult," "unmotivated," and "lazy". In truth he couldn't do the homework because he didn't know how. Your child may be avoiding homework for the same reason. Her brain may have internal challenges that you don't understand.

Testing Provides Valuable Insights

If your child really seems to struggle with classwork—learning to read, reading comprehension, written language, math concepts, learning math facts, etc.—then good testing can clear away the foggy suspicions. Good testing provides a clear picture of your child's strengths and weaknesses. That picture sets the foundation for understanding the kind of help and support your child needs to maximize his success as a learner.

Here are the most common sources of testing:

1. **Psychologists and neuropsychologists:** For most schools and colleges, a battery of cognitive tests must document your child's learning difference or disability in order to qualify a child to receive accommodations and academic support. Generally, either a psychologist or a neuropsychologist must administer these tests. If you go this route, be prepared for an investment of money and time. A good evaluation requires hours of testing and interpretation. Parents and teachers both will need to complete questionnaires. It takes many hours for the evaluator to analyze the results and write up a report and recommendations.

   Good evaluators won't just give you a bunch of test scores with numbers. They should be able to explain in clear language how these scores show your child's strengths and weaknesses. There should be a written set of recommendations for strategies, tools, and local professional resources. It should outline what to do next with this testing information. It should be a plan outlining how to support your child's development as a learner.

Interview any potential evaluators carefully to determine their experience testing children for learning disabilities. You are not looking for an IQ score. You are looking for a better understanding of why your child is struggling in school and what you can do to help her succeed.

2. **Speech pathologists, educational therapists, and learning specialists:** Most of these professionals have been trained to assess functions in their area of expertise. In most settings, their evaluations can contribute to, but may not be sufficient on their own to qualify a child for school accommodations. Their testing may be used to set up an educational intervention plan to address specific weaknesses. These professionals might do the actual remediation or supplemental education programs with your child.

Be sure to interview these professionals to determine their experience and qualifications for administering tests and providing services for remediation.

3. **Reading tutors:** These are professional tutors, often with a formal educational background, who are trained to assess children for reading competence. Their testing is usually done specifically to determine a child's areas of weakness connected only to the reading process. This testing is used to develop a targeted tutoring program to build the necessary skills to become a reader.

Reading tutors cannot diagnose dyslexia. That has to be done by a psychologist or neuropsychologist. Don't expect schools to make classroom accommodations or change their reading intervention program based on the testing results provided by a reading tutor.

As always, interview potential tutors and ask about their training using multisensory programs. What is their background? What is their experience? To learn more about dyslexia, investigate the website of the International Dyslexia Association: www.interdys.org.

You may be wondering why you would put your child through the testing process. Both of my children have had full batteries of cognitive testing. In both cases the information was very useful for everyone. My children understood themselves better, which guided them in their school and professional choices. As a parent I could see that their school struggles were based in the brain and were not the result of not trying hard enough.

 **Notepad**

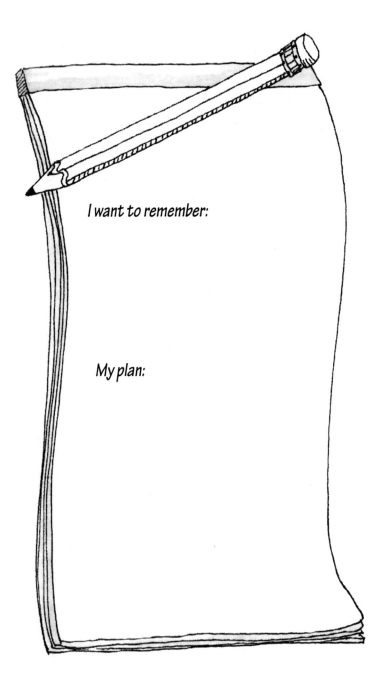

I want to remember:

My plan:

#42 *Anxiety or Depression?*

Struggles and failure in school can create a lot of complicated and troubling emotional responses in a child. The rates of anxiety and depression are on the rise in children, and I suspect it is in great part because schools and our society as a whole have placed unreasonable expectations on the executive capacity of our young people. We expect our children, adolescents, and young adults to function as if they have adult brains—brains that can manage the future, can easily delay gratification, can plan and execute projects that are due over an expanse of time, etc.

While more and more educators are becoming familiar with how to support children with EF weaknesses, not all teachers and schools (or parents, grandparents, and neighbors) are up to speed with current scientific research. In many situations children with EF weaknesses might still be told they are being "lazy" because of difficulties with production and output—getting homework and projects completed and turned in on time. Their "poor work habits," "poor time management," and "poor focus" are labeled as character flaws that need to be corrected by experiencing the consequences of their poor choices.

The truth is that many of these children are incapable, from a brain development perspective, of learning quickly from those negative consequences. I remember a really nice, bright sixteen-year-old telling his mother in one of our sessions, "Do you think that I like it when you keep taking the car away from me because I've got missing assignments? I don't do this on purpose!" Students with EF challenges may just keep failing, and all that failure hurts—a lot. They internalize that they are incompetent in learning situations. They give up, shut down, and escape. It is *really* hard to dig out of the mindset of being a failure.

If your child might be dealing with anxiety and depression, get help from more than one front.

1. **Find mental health support.** If you are worried about your child who has symptoms of anxiety, depression, or excessive outbursts of anger, seek the help of a professional who has the expertise to address these issues. Be courageous and ask for help. Do it now!

   Ask for referrals from school counselors, your pediatrician, and friends. Interview different providers to determine their experience and training for working with children who have your child's symptoms. It can take some searching to find a match for your child, but persevere. And don't expect instant results.

2. **Get academic support.** Get your child academic support outside of school if needed. Good educational therapists and tutors can help with explaining homework. They can help your child build missing academic skills so that she is more successful at meeting school expectations. Check out the resources in the appendix for websites to access educational therapists and trained reading tutors.

   If your finances are tight, check with your school to see if it has a peer-tutoring program. Some Boys & Girls Clubs have tutoring programs. You might be able to swap skills with a neighbor—he tutors your child, and you do an hour of errands or housekeeping for him. College students often make good tutors. Ask around for references and referrals.

3. Consider changing schools. Your child might thrive in a different setting. See tip #40 for more about choosing schools.

It can be so frustrating to watch your child struggle. It is painful beyond belief if your child fails spectacularly. I urge you to find help. Have courage. It is not about you; it is about helping your child learn about herself. It's about her developing skills for success.

 *Notepad*

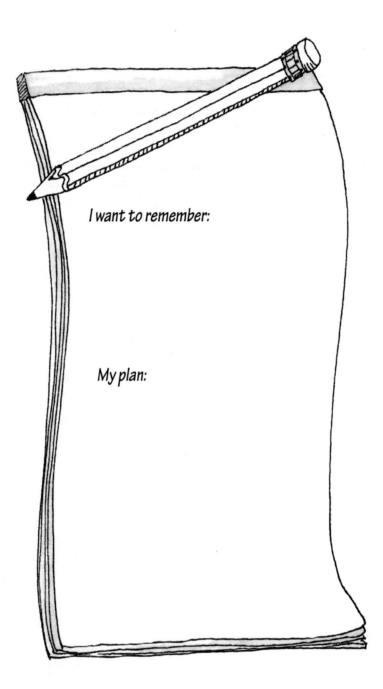

I want to remember:

My plan:

Addictions Old and New

#43

There was a time when alcohol and drugs were the only addictions on a parent's radar screen. These days we can add two more concerns: video games and smartphones. Like EF weaknesses, addictions get in the way of getting things done.

An addiction is a connection to a substance or behavior that has taken over the brain, bypassing the executive functions that control our behavior. People get sucked into addictions because they make them feel good.

If you have a child with significant EF weaknesses and he is struggling in school, it is a good idea to be watchful and take action as necessary. After all, with unsupported executive functions, a child might easily engage in behaviors that provide him an escape from the discomfort and guilt associated with not getting things done and letting people down.

Escape Behaviors

If you are concerned that your child is using a substance or behavior to escape the demands of reality, take action! People need help to end addictive behaviors.

1. **Drugs and alcohol:** Don't mess around if you suspect drug and alcohol use by your child. Get help *now*. There are mental health counselors who specialize in

this area. Pediatricians and school counselors should be able to provide local resources.

2. **Video games:** Excessive gaming can become a serious problem if game time is interfering with interacting with people in person or meeting the responsibilities of daily life. Tons of money, time, and brain research goes into designing these games so that people won't stop playing them. It is a real setup for those with EF weaknesses, because in the gaming world, they can be masterful and competent—unlike their experiences in the real world.

   If you are concerned about your child's gaming habits, look for a mental health practitioner in your area who specializes with youth and gaming addictions. They exist!

3. **Smartphones:** Have you heard of the "Heads-Down Generation?" Observe a bunch of teens waiting at a bus stop, and you'll instantly understand where the phrase came from. Excessive smartphone usage is causing concerns in many circles. Researchers are actively investigating the impact of excessive cell phone use on brain development and social interactions. The South Korean government is so concerned about smartphone addiction in their young people that it is creating programs to help children break their addiction to their phones!

   I'm not sure if we have mental health providers already specializing in this problem. You'll need to check your local area. Talking with counselors who specialize in addictions of any kind would be a good place to start.

Smartphone-Free Zones

If you worry about your child's excessive connection to her phone, creating "smartphone-free zones" around your child might be a good idea for at least parts of the day. You might rule out phones at dinner or in the car while going to and from school or sports. I mention the car because it is often during those transition times that children will do the most in-person talking. There is something about riding in the car that opens them up. It's a great time to connect and find out what is going on in your child's world. Tips #32 and #33 also address cell phone issues.

 *Notepad*

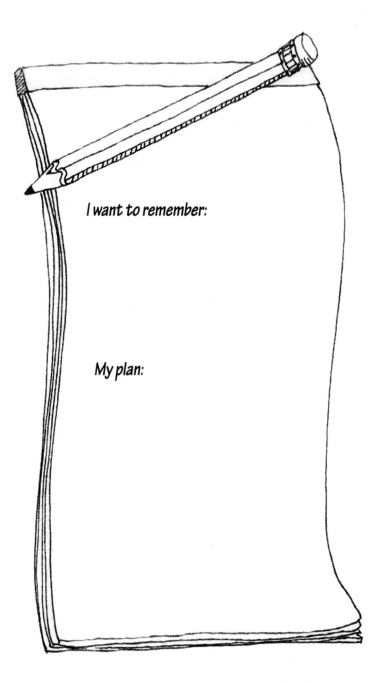

I want to remember:

My plan:

Sleep Deprivation

For many children turning out the lights and saying goodnight does not mean that child is actually going to fall asleep quickly and easily. Lying awake for an extended period of time creates inadequate sleep, which has a negative impact on executive functioning the next day. It impacts mood and the brain's energy and ability to focus on new learning during the school day. And it turns out that a good night's sleep is a critical part of learning, as the brain consolidates memories and experiences during sleep cycles.

Parents can help by guiding their child to establish good sleep hygiene. Sleep hygiene simply refers to the habits that set up good sleep patterns, which include consistent times for both going to bed and getting out of bed. Search *sleep hygiene* on the web to learn more.

However, some of those online references leave out an important contributor to "not feeling sleepy at bedtime": the light coming out of our electronic devices.

Screen Time and Sleep

Avoid looking at device screens before bedtime. The spectrum of light emitted from our computer screens, tablets, and smartphones messes up the development of melatonin that naturally builds up in our brain as night falls. It is melatonin that helps us feel sleepy. Avoiding screens in the thirty minutes to an hour before bedtime can calm down some of those "activated" adolescents who can't fall asleep easily. Tip #33 also talks about how teen sleep is being disrupted by cell phones.

If your child has sleep issues, I recommend reading *Snooze or Lose* by Dr. Helene Emsellem.

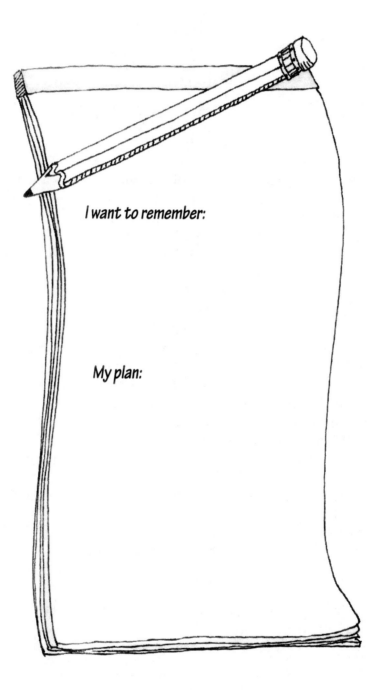

I want to remember:

My plan:

Learned Helplessness

Children who cannot work independently without someone right next to them "helping" them all the time can develop what is called "learned helplessness." These children believe that they are incompetent and unable to succeed at tasks on their own. They lack the experience of being self-competent, and they're often labeled as "lazy" or "unmotivated." They are frozen in their experience of being incompetent when on their own.

It is critical for children with learned helplessness to develop an internal belief in their own competency. The only way to reach that competency is to experience independent success based upon their *own effort*.

Undoing this learned helplessness requires a parent with a plan and a lot of patience. You must start very small and build, one step at a time, to decrease dependence so gradually that the child isn't even aware of the separation as it is happening.

The best description I've found for overcoming learned helplessness is in the book *The Motivation Breakthrough* by Richard Lavoie. This is an excellent book for helping you understand motivation. If you have a child with motivation issues, especially learned helplessness, I recommend that you read it.

I loved Lavoie's approach so much that I've included an adaptation of it in tip #34. It is an excellent description of how to teach a child to do a task well and independently.

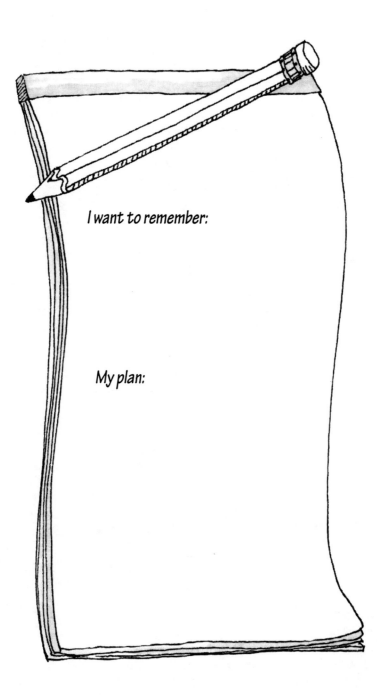

I want to remember:

My plan:

ten

My Final Tips

Up to this point in the book, most of the tips have been suggestions for ways to compensate for your child's weaknesses in executive function skills. They help you change the environment to provide external reminders of what to do. These last tips are more for you, the parent.

The first tip in this chapter is a gift from my mother. I never liked learning it as a child, but I am so glad she took the time to repeat it over and over and over again so that I learned it. It was one of her lasting gifts to me.

The second two tips come from my years of being a parent and years of supporting struggling, concerned parents. The fourth tip comes from my heart. I hope you will find room for it in yours. And the final tip is about how to best use this book now that you own it.

Such Is Life

Such is life. Those were my mother's words. Whenever I whined and complained about having to do something I didn't want to do, she would turn and look at me and say, "Honey, such is life. You better get used to it." In a gentle, firm way, she was building a key aspect of my executive functions that helped me get around my brain's other EF weaknesses. She was helping me to learn to control my own impulsive desires and behaviors by delaying my need for instant gratification. This ability to control one's own desires by putting work before play is the foundation of a good work ethic. While it may seem boring and old-fashioned, a good work ethic is critical to becoming a successful and independent adult.

Not All of Life Will Be Fun

There's a point in my "Seeing My Time" course where I have parents and children read aloud a sentence with me. I tell them to put special emphasis on the words *don't want to do*.

Here's the sentence:

Life requires doing things that you *don't want to do*, on time and to the best of your ability.

All of us have things that we don't want to do. Parents don't want to do dishes, vacuum, pay bills, do laundry, prepare taxes, etc. Children don't want to do homework or chores. And yet if we do these things, on time and to the best of our ability, our lives will work! Conflicts will diminish. You'll be able to fix dinner in a clean kitchen. The house won't be embarrassingly messy or dirty. You won't pay late fees on bills. You won't have late taxes hanging over your head for months or years. There will be clean soccer socks when your child needs them. Your child's homework will be done on time. You won't be getting those awful emails from teachers. And you will be able to appreciate the fact that your child is helping around the house instead of yelling at her for not pulling her weight and being helpful.

Work Before Play

It's so sad when I come across kids (and some adults) who just want to have fun all the time. They fight anything connected to "work" and "have-to-dos." Life isn't going to be easy for these folks. It won't be easy for the people around them either.

I'm not against having fun. I set my time up to be sure that I do have fun—after my work gets done!

Building a work ethic will set your child on the road to success. Support him in learning how to do what he doesn't want to do. He will thank you in the end.

 *Notepad*

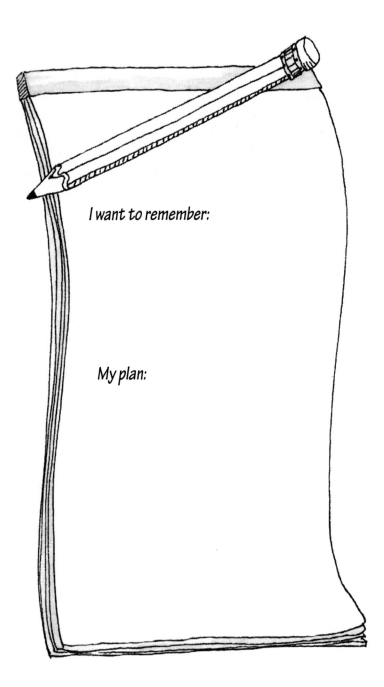

I want to remember:

My plan:

Have Patience

One of the few good things about getting older is the perspective it provides regarding children and parenting. Short of serious health concerns, nothing is more stressful or painful than having a child who is struggling in school.

You picked up this book looking for ways to help your child. These tips, if practiced over time, will indeed help. However, I want to remind you of the words from the first chapter: little by little, change happens.

Remember too that the brain's executive functions don't fully develop until a person is thirty or more years old! Depending on your child's age, that's probably a long time from now. This is where patience comes in handy.

Provide Practice and Support

While you are waiting for that mature brain to come on board, your job is to keep the tools and strategies you learn from this book in front of your child. You need to continuously provide practice and support until habits of good time management, planning, and organization are automatic for your child. She will grow up. Honest. It just takes time and patience.

I've been doing this work long enough to have seen some seriously wobbling children and adolescents transition into independent, capable adults. Each child has his own timeline for brain development. Each will have individual strengths and weaknesses.

The time you invest in helping your child build her executive skills will give her the option of meeting her full adult potential. It just takes time, practice, and patience.

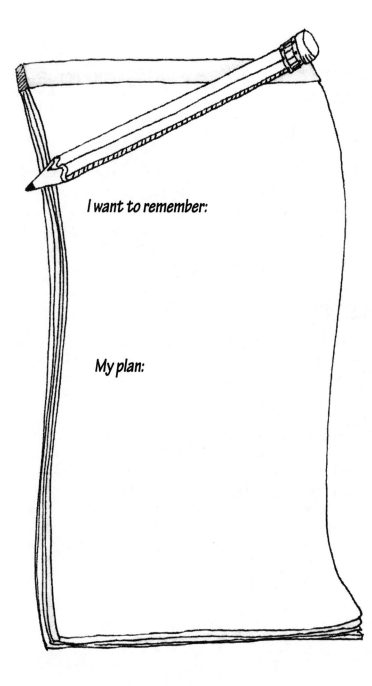

I want to remember:

My plan:

Plan a Play Date

It is really easy to get caught up in worry and frustration when you have a child struggling in school. For some parents it is a constant battle—with the child, his teachers, the school, even his other parent. It is exhausting too. You probably have other roles and responsibilities that need your time, attention, and energy.

Give Yourselves a Treat

Don't forget to enjoy your child, especially if you feel like you are living in battle mode. Set up a "play date" for you and your child, no matter her age. Put it on your calendar. Put it on her calendar too, and then be sure that you do it.

The play date doesn't have to be a big deal. What you want to do is to create a little bubble of positive experience together. Don't bring up school. Don't go near sensitive, painful topics. Just enjoy doing something together, even if it is as simple as going out for an ice-cream cone—just the two of you. The more positive memories you create, the easier it will be for you to get through the tough stuff.

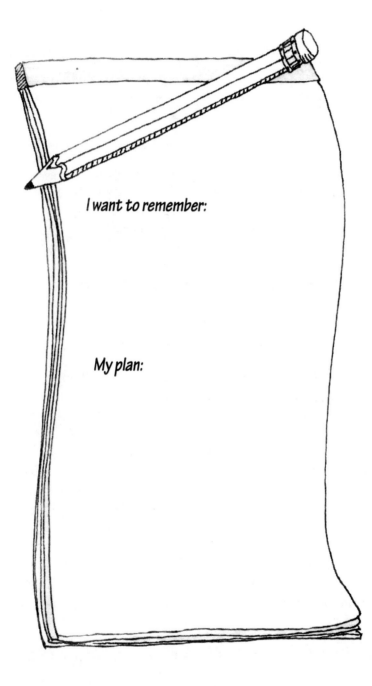

I want to remember:

My plan:

#49 *From My Heart to Yours*

Being a parent can be really hard and sometimes lonely work. Children don't come with directions. In our culture we don't receive much support or training for what can be the most demanding job of our lives. Perhaps, like us, you are raising your children miles and miles away from extended family. Or perhaps you have an extended family that isn't such a great source of advice or support. You might be going it completely alone as a single parent. So we parents muddle along, read a few books, listen to our peers, and make mistakes—sometimes lots of them.

My children keep telling me that I did many things right as a parent. I also know that I made some mistakes and wish I could do a few things over again for them. When I was raising my children, parents didn't know about the executive functions of the brain and how they impact behavior. In my ignorance, when confronted with missing assignments, procrastination, messy rooms, and undone chores, I was quick to blame and condemn the behaviors as a lack of willpower, poor motivation, laziness, ungratefulness, etc. Threats and consequences multiplied but were ineffective. It wasn't pretty. I know now that I was inadvertently contributing to setting up more struggle and failure for them. And that knowledge hurts.

When you have a child who struggles and experiences failure, you feel his pain as well as your own pain. You also feel like a failure. So much emotion can boil up and over for the whole family. Some of that emotion may be anger—anger at yourself and at your child.

Unresolved Anger Isn't Healthy

If you're feeling anger over your child's struggles or failure, I urge you to pause and take a deep breath. Unresolved anger gets in the way of growth for both the child and the parent. I advise you to get some help to let it go.

Be Kinder to Yourself and Your Child

It is easy to feel like a victim of your child's choices and behaviors. Stop. It is not about you. You've been doing the best you could do with the knowledge you had. Your child is doing the best that she can with the brain and parents that she was given.

Forgiveness Is Powerful

It was a wonderful day for me when I realized the obvious. I had to forgive myself for being a less-than-perfect parent. I also had to forgive my children for being less than perfect. I had to let go and accept us as we are—pretty amazing, hard-working, and lovable people—who are not and never will be perfect. I'm thankful to be able to say that, based on that forgiveness, we have all blossomed into very capable and competent adults, despite our inherent weaknesses with executive functioning.

Failure Is Part of Learning

Of course we want our children to be successful at whatever they undertake. And because we feel their pain when they fail, we are motivated to try to protect our children from failure. However, it is true that we learn from our mistakes. We need to remind our children that we become stronger, wiser, smarter, as we face and overcome challenges. Learning to manage setbacks will help your child build the resiliency that life requires. A few skinned knees and a few bouts with failing are often the underpinnings of learning, personal growth, and ultimately success.

I recommend that you read *Mindset*, by Carol Dweck. Her research will change how you view challenges and failures. It may also change how you speak to your child. It is one of those books I wish had been available when my children were growing up. It would have helped me be a better parent.

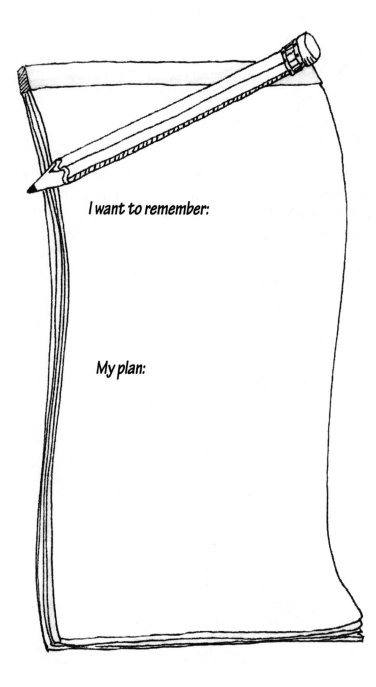

I want to remember:

My plan:

#50 *What to Do Next*

The best way to build your child's executive function skills for success in school and life is to not put this book on a bookshelf. If you do, it will go out of sight and out of mind, and you may only benefit from a tip or two.

How to Get the Maximum from This Book

1. **Keep this book near you.** I suggest you keep this book with you for a while and in sight as you work with different tips to solve different problems. Look at it often.
2. **Create reminders.** Another way to remember to read more tips is to create reminders on your paper or electronic calendar.
3. **Share this book with others.** Discuss what you have learned from this book with other parents. Share your own stories and your own tips for helping your children develop their executive function skills.

Be Proud of Yourself

Congratulations on reading this book. I wish you the very best on your journey to help your child build her time-management, planning, and organizational skills. By reading this book, you are acting as a great model for your child. You are showing her the value of learning and the importance of respecting the development of our amazing brain.

You are teaching your child critical life skills. Well done!

Remember—little by little, change happens. Little by little, your child will grow into adult independence. Breathe.

If You Have Enjoyed This Book

I invite you to visit my website and sign up for my newsletter. Along with my blogs, it contains more tips and bits of knowledge I love to share. Staying in touch with me will help you remember to use your tools and strategies so that they can become habits. www.ExecutiveFunctioning Success.com.

 *Notepad*

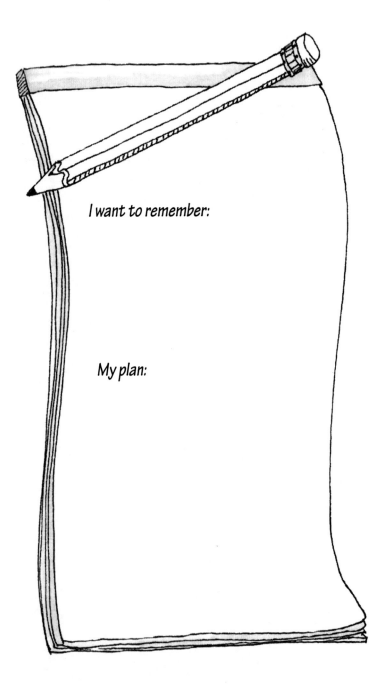

I want to remember:

My plan:

appendix

Appendix: The Extras

Appendix I

Evaluating Executive Function Skills: Your Child's and Yours

Our brain's executive functions are so complex that there isn't one tidy definition of what executive functions are and what they do. Different researchers from different disciplines all have their own list of significant skills. Some descriptions are very brief, others extremely complex. With a little tweaking on my part, the model that I find the best to use is one put forth by Peg Dawson and Richard Guare. After you've read this book, I recommend you investigate their books, which are listed in the resources section on page 217. They have titles for both parents and professionals.

Understand Your Child's Brain and Yours

Following are descriptions of the eleven EF skills from Dawson and Guare's model. As you read them, consider your child's brain and behavior. Ask yourself if the listed EF skill is a strength or weakness for your child. In some instances you might decide that it's both a strength and a weakness, depending upon the circumstance. For example, a child might be good at starting something that she likes to do (the EF skill of task initiation) but procrastinate over homework or chores. I encourage you to also think about your own brain and behavior. Which of the EF skills are your strengths, and which are your weaknesses?

At the end of the description for each EF skill, there is a place to record whether this EF skill merits a plus or a minus. If it is a strength, mark it "+." If it is a weakness, mark it a "-." It is also possible to have a "+/-" depending upon the situation. Rate your child first and then yourself. Once completed, this will give you the big picture of your child's struggles and perhaps your own. Add up the pluses and minuses for each of you. The more executive functioning weaknesses a person has, the harder it is to produce—to get things done on time.

The "Big Three" of Our EF System

While all EF skills are part of a complex executive system, metacognition, working memory, and emotional control are what I call the "Big Three." I say this because if you have a weakness in any of these three key areas, then many of your executive functions are diminished.

METACOGNITION

Metacognition is a big word representing a big concept. When I ask families who come to see me if they know the definition of *metacognition*, I usually get shaking heads and blank looks. Don't worry, I only learned this word a few years back, but I always tell my families that metacognition is *powerful*. By the time they finish my course, *metacognition* becomes their favorite new word. I had a fourth grader gleefully report, "Marydee, my metacognition is getting better!"

Metacognition is an awareness of your learning and thinking processes. It is often described as being able to "think about your thinking." This is a pretty complex, mind-bending idea, but it is critical to develop. The key to changing habits and behaviors is to develop your metacognition—your self-awareness as well as your ability to pause, self-reflect, analyze your choices, and learn from your mistakes.

I help people think about metacognition in a couple of ways. It is a little like having an out-of-body experience, watching your behavior, asking yourself why you did something, and wondering how you could have done it differently to reach a better outcome. It is a little like having a conversation with yourself in your mind.

For children, I describe it as having an angel on one shoulder and the devil on the other. The angel says, "Time to start my homework." And then the devil says, "Oh, I'll start later. I'll just finish this level of my video game."

Many young children, and even those much older, are beings who just respond immediately to what is in front of them or around them. They don't pause to consider outcomes or discuss choices in their minds. Their brains simply have not yet developed that capacity. Children with ADHD and those on the autism spectrum can have difficulty pausing to self-reflect on their choices and independently develop their metacognition. They need help, guidance, and patience to develop this critical executive skill. This is where you come in. You need to coach your child to pause and reflect on choices.

My Child's Brain:____ My Brain:____

WORKING MEMORY

The impact of deficits in working memory on our ability to get things done and to learn is huge. For our purposes, I'm going to simplify a very complicated aspect of our brain. I think of our working memory as that part of our brain where we are consciously thinking. As you read and understand this, you are using your working memory.

As I wrote in the introduction to chapter three, there are two important things to know about working memory. First, it can't hold much information at one time. Second, it doesn't last very long. It's like writing on a sticky note. An average adult's working memory can manage five to seven chunks of information at a time. It is as if all your "thinking" must fit on a 3X3 sticky note. A child has even less working memory. However, what you are thinking about is not going to stay put for very long, because working memory only holds onto things for seconds. It is as if there is an automatic delete button. After a few seconds, it gets pushed and poof, our thoughts are gone. With a limited working memory capacity like mine, which handles three to four bits at a time, you are functioning with the smallest sticky note. With that little sticky note's worth of working memory, it is really easy to forget things, lose things, have trouble following directions, forget to turn things in, fail to keep up with and contribute to group discussions, shy away from doing math calculations in your head, or stare blankly at complicated, multistep tasks like reading, math, and organizing writing for essays. Does this sound like your child? Does this sound like you?

The reason that working memory is one of the Big Three executive functions is that, like metacognition, working memory affects many of the other executive skills in the brain. Working memory limits the capacity of the brain to manage multiple things at once. Poor working memory capacity can interfere with efficiency and might look like forgetfulness or inattention.

*My Child's Brain:*____ *My Brain:*____

EMOTIONAL CONTROL

When it comes to executive function skills, controlling emotions is unique in its power. I call this EF skill the "bully in the brain." Strong emotions, like anger, fear, anxiety, depression, frustration, and even falling in love, can dominate our thinking and wipe out our access to using our other executive skills. When a strong emotion is triggered, our emotional response floods over our whole body and our mind. We feel that strong emotion, and it can block out our thinking brain—our ability to use meta-cognition to calmly problem solve, focus, get started, etc. This is why you can't reason with a child or adult who is angry or upset. They have lost the power to control their thinking and their behavior.

My Child's Brain:____ My Brain:____

Eight Other Critical Executive Skills

SUSTAINED ATTENTION

Sustained attention refers to the ability to stay focused on a task so that you can complete it. If your mind wanders all the time and you are easily distracted, then your brain has a weakness in this area. Interestingly, however, the ability to stay focused can be scored as a +/-, because for some people—those with ADHD, for instance—their ability to stay focused will depend upon the circumstances. If something is novel, dangerous, exciting, or challenging, they can stay focused or even hyper-focus. If the task is boring or repetitious, then their minds will wander. This explains the child who can focus for hours on a video game but can't focus on a sheet of math facts.

My Child's Brain:____ My Brain:____

GOAL-DIRECTED PERSISTENCE

Goal-directed persistence refers to your ability to stick

with things to finish them. Becoming good at playing an instrument requires goal-directed persistence to do the necessary practice. If you or your child have lots of unfinished projects, then you have challenges in this area of executive functioning. Your score on this one can also depend upon the task or circumstances. You might be good at finishing the things you like to do and not so good at finishing what you don't like to do. In this case you'd get a +/- score for goal-directed persistence.

My Child's Brain:____ My Brain:____

MENTAL FLEXIBILITY

Mental flexibility describes your brain's ability to go with the flow, to change direction easily and quickly when circumstances change unexpectedly. It's the ability to try a different approach to solving a difficult problem. It's connected to the ability to see more than one point of view. Children who have a difficult time transitioning from one activity to another are exhibiting a lack of mental flexibility. Those who have challenges with mental flexibility like order and predictability. Spontaneous changes upset them. Individuals on the autism spectrum often have challenges with this EF skill.

My Child's Brain:____ My Brain:____

RESPONSE INHIBITION OR SELF-REGULATION

Response inhibition is the ability to control your responses to the environment around you. It is your internal ability to self-regulate or control your own behavior. Is your child able to pause and think before she acts? Or does your child constantly get into trouble for speaking out or doing things when she shouldn't? Can she delay gratification and stop playing a video game when she needs to work? Does she do dangerous things without thinking because they sounded exciting and fun? Response inhibition means having a brain that can pause to allow you to use metacognition and think about the best, smartest action to take next. It's a brain that can say no and stop you from doing something that may have a negative consequence.

My Child's Brain:___ My Brain:___

TIME MANAGEMENT

Yes, time management is a specific executive function skill. For me, time management means two things. First, do you have the ability to use your time well? Do you work when you need to work and play later? Or do you play when you should be working? Are you on time, or are you always late and rushed?

The second way I think about time management is to ask if you have an internal clock. Are you conscious of time passing? There seem to be two kinds of people: those who have an internal clock and those who don't. I don't. As the day progresses, I don't have any idea how much time I spend doing something. I don't know if fifteen minutes have passed or an hour. I've gone on vacation and lost days. Once it was Thursday and I thought it was Tuesday!

My Child's Brain:___ My Brain:___

PLANNING AND PRIORITIZING

This is the executive skill required to get projects done. Being able to plan and prioritize enables us to reach complex future goals, such as completing school projects, applying to college, completing college courses, writing books, building a business, and planning vacations. Being able to plan and prioritize helps us meet deadlines.

Can you or your child take a big project that is due in the future—a few weeks out or further—and figure out how to break it into chunks so that you get it done on time with a minimum of stress? Can you figure out the important place to start? Or are projects put off to the last minute? Is too much time spent on the fun part of the project so that there isn't time for working on the harder parts?

My Child's Brain:____ My Brain:____

ORGANIZATION

The EF skill of being able to organize ties into two key areas: objects and our thinking. It is easiest to think about objects, since that usually means "stuff." If your child's desk, room, backpack, or locker is a mess of piles where things are constantly getting lost and misplaced, then he has a deficit in organization.

The thinking aspect of organization is trickier and not so obvious; however, it can be at the root of not starting or completing writing assignments. The task of writing makes heavy demands upon multiple executive skills, including organization.

My Child's Brain:____ My Brain:____

TASK INITIATION

The formal term for being able to get started on something is referred to as "task initiation." Task initiation is another critical executive function skill of the brain. If a child gets stuck because she doesn't know how to start or is always putting things off, then she has a problem with this executive skill. People who put things off are labeled "procrastinators." There are lots of different reasons for procrastinating, and various tips in this book address those different reasons. Right now it is important to know that you can get a +/- score for this EF skill because the ability to get started often depends upon the task. It is easy to start something you like to do, but not so easy to start something you don't like to do.

My Child's Brain:____ My Brain:____

Putting It All Together

You have now scored both your child and yourself on the strengths and weaknesses of your executive skills. Total up your scores.

My Child: Strengths ____ Weaknesses ____ Combination _____

Myself: Strengths ____ Weaknesses ____ Combination _____

Now that you have this picture, you have a better understanding of the role of EF in your child's struggles. And perhaps you learned the roots of your own struggles.

I hope this begins to change how you think about your child's often frustrating behavior. You can't do what your brain can't do. If your child has multiple deficits in specific executive skills, then she is going to have even greater challenges in getting things done. The more weaknesses, the harder it is to control your time management, planning, and organizing. If your child falls into this category, then he is going to need lots of external support to make up for what the brain can't do internally.

What Are External Supports?

I think of external supports in a couple of different ways. An external support is a tool that is used to solve a problem. For instance, I am short, and to reach things on upper shelves, I need help. I can use a stepstool, or I can ask someone who is taller to get the object I need. In the first option, I'm problem solving and deciding to use a tool that I've used in the past when I was too short to reach something. In using the second option, asking for help, I'm taking advantage of another person's ability or strength that I don't have. In both of these examples, I am using metacognition.

While your child's brain is maturing, you are going to need to lend your child the strengths of your mature executive functioning. You are going to have to support her, guide her, and coach her in how to develop the metacognition to build her own grown-up brain. You need to provide the tools and strategies to build good time-management skills, which are critical for success and satisfaction. You are going to be one of her critical external supports.

How Do You Help?

With the tips in this book, I've shown you how to build that metacognition. I've given you suggestions for tools and strategies to solve the most common challenges your child faces when it comes to getting things done for school and around the house. These tips will all tie back to the brain and its executive functions—the strengths and weakness each of us have.

Remember: There Is No Magic Wand

The families I've worked with have all found relief in using the tools, strategies, and tips I am sharing with you in this book. However, they also learned that the key is to be patient. Changing your child's behavior is going to take repetition, practice, and coaching reminders. Over time he will need your support less and less. The key idea here is *over time*. Rather than being angry or frustrated with your child, be realistic. Enjoy watching your child master these tools and strategies. Celebrate together as he learns to get things done independently. All sorts of wonders come from being able to manage your time so that you can reach goals and dreams. Give your child this gift, the life skill of time management. Remember: little by little, change happens.

Appendix II

Resources

PARENTING

Dweck, C. 2007. *Mindset: The New Psychology of Success.* New York: Ballantine Books.

Emsellem, H. 2006. *Snooze...or Lose! 10 "No-War" Ways to Improve Your Teen's Sleep Habits.* Washington, DC: Joseph Henry Press.

Lavoie, R. 2007. *The Motivation Breakthrough: 6 Secrets to Turning On the Tuned-Out Child.* New York: Touchstone.

Masarie, K., et al. 2009. *Raising Our Sons: The Ultimate Parenting Guide for Healthy Boys and Strong Families.* Portland: Family Empowerment Network.

Masarie, K., et al. 2009. *Raising Our Daughters: The Ultimate Parenting Guide for Healthy Girls and Thriving Families.* Portland: Family Empowerment Network.

Walsh, D. 2007. *NO: Why Kids—of All Ages—Need to Hear It and Ways Parents Can Say It.* New York: Free Press.

EXECUTIVE FUNCTIONS EXPLAINED FOR PARENTS

Cooper-Kahn, J., and Dietzel, L. 2008. *Late, Lost, and Unprepared: A Parent's Guide to Helping Children with Executive Functioning.* Bethesda, MD: Woodbine House.

Cox, A. 2007. *No Mind Left Behind: Understanding and Fostering Executive Control—The Eight Essential Brain Skills Every Child Needs to Thrive.* New York: Penguin.

Dawson, P., and Guare, R. 2009. *Smart but Scattered: The Revolutionary "Executive Skills" Approach to Helping Children Reach Their Potential.* New York: The Guilford Press.

Dawson, P., and Guare, R. 2012. *Smart but Scattered Teens: The "Executive Skills" Program for Helping Children Reach Their Potential.* New York: The Guilford Press.

EXECUTIVE FUNCTIONS EXPLAINED FOR TEACHERS

Cooper-Kahn, J. and Foster, M. 2013. *Boosting Executive Skills in the Classroom: A Practical Guide for Educators.* San Francisco: Jossey-Bass.

Dawson, P., and Guare, R. 2010. *Executive Skills in Children and Adolescents: A Practical Guide to Assessment and Intervention,* 2nd ed. New York: The Guilford Press.

Kaufman, C. 2010. *Executive Function in the Classroom: Practical Strategies for Improving Performance and Enhancing Skills for All Students.* Baltimore: Paul H. Brooks Publishing.

WEBSITES FOR ADDITIONAL INFORMATION

The Association of Educational Therapists
www.aetonline.org
> Provides information on educational therapy and lists trained educational therapists to assist those struggling with learning.

CHADD
www.chadd.org
> Nationally recognized authority on ADHD.

Dr. David Walsh
www.drdavewalsh.com
> Resources and blogs for "mind-positive parenting."

Executive Functioning Success
www.ExecutiveFunctioningSuccess.com
> Marydee Sklar's website has additional blog tips on supporting EF skills, videos on relevant topics, and

links to Cool Tools to support time management, plus access to information about The Sklar Process® and the "Seeing My Time" courses for families, individuals, and schools.

The International Dyslexia Association
www.interdys.org
Provides resources for professionals and families dealing with individuals with reading disabilities. The national website and the state branches all have listings of tutors trained to help those with dyslexia.

LearnNet
www.projectlearnet.org
This is a great resource for information about the brain in general and for supporting those with brain injuries. Information for teachers, clinicians, parents, and students.

ABOUT THE AUTHOR

As an educator, Marydee Sklar has helped families and individuals overcome struggles with time management for almost twenty years. She teaches workshops on executive functions for professional and school communities, and can be booked to speak at events. She is the creator of the Sklar Process®—Much More Than Time Management and is the author of the Seeing My Time books. She lives in Portland, Oregon, with her husband, and Ubi the Queen Kitty.

ABOUT THE ILLUSTRATOR

Claire Ackerman McCrann has been delighting friends with her drawings for many years. This is her first book illustration project. She lives in Murrieta, California, with her husband, two part-time children, and two big dogs. Who knew that twenty-four years of embellishing Christmas letters with a family cartoon would start a career?

Also from Marydee:

THE SEEING MY TIME BOOKS

The Seeing My Time book series provides resources for everyone who needs them: educators, therapists, parents, students, and adults. With these resources, children and adults learn to master time management, planning, and organization, whether their executive function challenges stem from ADHD, Autism Spectrum Disorders, dyslexia, minimal traumatic brain injury, or some other obstacle that keeps them from realizing their potential.

Order at www.ExecutiveFunctioningSuccess.com.

FOR STUDENTS
Seeing My Time—Visual Tools for Executive Functioning Success
A series of multisensory activities corresponding to the six units of the "Seeing My Time" course, this workbook presents the lessons individuals need for building executive functioning skills in a fun, hands-on format. It becomes a valued permanent journal and reference tool.

FOR PROFESSIONALS
Seeing My Time—Instructor's Manual
Learn to teach the Seeing My Time course and help students and adults build executive functioning skills for life. This award-winning manual prepares professionals to direct participants through each page of the *Seeing My Time—Visual Tools for Executive Functioning Success* workbook.

FOR PARENTS
50 Tips to Help Students Succeed: Develop Your Student's Time-Management and Executive Skills for Life
This informative and practical book helps parents understand the executive function challenges their children and teens experience. Then it provides fifty quick, easy, and concrete strategies for parents to help their students succeed in school and life while minimizing stress and conflict. For best results, pair this book with the "Seeing My Time" course and workbook.

Work with Marydee:

Marydee Sklar and her team at Executive Functioning Success are dedicated to improving lives with the Sklar Process® – Much More Than Time Management.

PRIVATE AND GROUP SEEING MY TIME COURSES
For those struggling with poor time management, planning and organization. Suitable for ages eleven through adult. Available in person or live distance sessions.

For more information visit: http://executivefunctioning success.com/courses/

PROFESSIONAL TRAINING AND CERTIFICATION PROGRAM FOR TEACHING THE SKLAR PROCESS
Designed for those professionals who assist clients, students, or employees who struggle with the executive functions of time management, planning, and organization. Useful for educators, educational therapists, speech pathologists, psychologists, counselors, and managers.

For more information visit: http://executivefunctioning success.com/courses/

CONSULTING FOR EDUCATIONAL SETTINGS
Programs to educate faculty about the connection between the brain's executive functions and student success. Appropriate

for elementary through university programs. Options include integrating the Seeing My Time curriculum into the student support services of schools, colleges, and universities.

For more information visit: http://executivefunctioning success.com/school-intro/

CONSULTING FOR BUSINESS SETTINGS

Programs for managers and employees to develop an understanding of how the brain's executive functions connect to productivity, being on time, time management, planning, and organization. Valuable for all levels of management and employees, especially those responsible for team projects and employee support.

For more information visit: http://executivefunctioning success.com/companies-organizations-intro/

CPSIA information can be obtained
at www.ICGtesting.com
Printed in the USA
FFOW02n0910310518
46859101-49071FF